WOMEN IN CANADIAN POLITICS

*This is Volume 6 in a series of studies
commissioned as part of the research program
of the Royal Commission on Electoral Reform
and Party Financing*

WOMEN IN CANADIAN POLITICS
TOWARD EQUITY IN REPRESENTATION

Kathy Megyery
Editor

Volume 6 of the Research Studies

ROYAL COMMISSION ON ELECTORAL REFORM
AND PARTY FINANCING
AND CANADA COMMUNICATION GROUP –
PUBLISHING, SUPPLY AND SERVICES CANADA

DUNDURN PRESS
TORONTO AND OXFORD

© Minister of Supply and Services Canada, 1991
Printed and bound in Canada
ISBN 1-55002-102-8
ISSN 1188-2743
Catalogue No. Z1-1989/2-41-6E

Published by Dundurn Press Limited in cooperation with the Royal Commission on Electoral Reform and Party Financing and Canada Communication Group – Publishing, Supply and Services Canada.

Canadian Cataloguing in Publication Data

Main entry under title:
Women in Canadian politics

(Research studies ; 6)
Issued also in French under title: Les Femmes et la politique canadienne.
ISBN 1-55002-102-8

1. Women in politics – Canada. 2. Politicians – Canada. I. Megyery, Kathy, 1962– . II. Canada. Royal Commission on Electoral Reform and Party Financing. III. Series: Research studies (Canada. Royal Commission on Electoral Reform and Party Financing) ; 6.

HQ1391.C3W64 1991   305.43'32'0971   C91-090518-5

Dundurn Press Limited
2181 Queen Street East
Suite 301
Toronto, Canada
M4E 1E5

Dundurn Distribution
73 Lime Walk
Headington
Oxford, England
0X3 7AD

CONTENTS

FIGURES

TABLES

3. LEGISLATIVE TURNOVER AND THE ELECTION OF WOMEN TO THE CANADIAN HOUSE OF COMMONS

4. WOMEN AND CANDIDACIES FOR THE HOUSE OF COMMONS

FOREWORD

THE ROYAL COMMISSION on Electoral Reform and Party Financing was established in November 1989. Our mandate was to inquire into and report on the appropriate principles and process that should govern the election of members of the House of Commons and the financing of political parties and candidates' campaigns. To conduct such a comprehensive examination of Canada's electoral system, we held extensive public consultations and developed a research program designed to ensure that our recommendations would be guided by an independent foundation of empirical inquiry and analysis.

The Commission's in-depth review of the electoral system was the first of its kind in Canada's history of electoral democracy. It was dictated largely by the major constitutional, social and technological changes of the past several decades, which have transformed Canadian society, and their concomitant influence on Canadians' expectations of the political process itself. In particular, the adoption in 1982 of the *Canadian Charter of Rights and Freedoms* has heightened Canadians' awareness of their democratic and political rights and of the way they are served by the electoral system.

The importance of electoral reform cannot be overemphasized. As the Commission's work proceeded, Canadians became increasingly preoccupied with constitutional issues that have the potential to change the nature of Confederation. No matter what their beliefs or political allegiances in this continuing debate, Canadians agree that constitutional change must be achieved in the context of fair and democratic processes. We cannot complacently assume that our current electoral process will always meet this standard or that it leaves no room for improvement. Parliament and the national government must be seen as legitimate; electoral reform can both enhance the stature of national political institutions and reinforce their ability to define the future of our country in ways that command Canadians' respect and confidence and promote the national interest.

In carrying out our mandate, we remained mindful of the importance of protecting our democratic heritage, while at the same time balancing it against the emerging values that are injecting a new dynamic into the electoral system. If our system is to reflect the realities of Canadian political life, then reform requires more than mere tinkering with electoral laws and practices.

Our broad mandate challenged us to explore a full range of options. We commissioned more than 100 research studies, to be published in a 23-volume collection. In the belief that our electoral laws must measure up to the very best contemporary practice, we examined election-related laws and processes in all of our provinces and territories and studied comparable legislation and processes in established democracies around the world. This unprecedented array of empirical study and expert opinion made a vital contribution to our deliberations. We made every effort to ensure that the research was both intellectually rigorous and of practical value. All studies were subjected to peer review, and many of the authors discussed their preliminary findings with members of the political and academic communities at national symposiums on major aspects of the electoral system.

The Commission placed the research program under the able and inspired direction of Dr. Peter Aucoin, Professor of Political Science and Public Administration at Dalhousie University. We are confident that the efforts of Dr. Aucoin, together with those of the research coordinators and scholars whose work appears in this and other volumes, will continue to be of value to historians, political scientists, parliamentarians and policy makers, as well as to thoughtful Canadians and the international community.

Along with the other Commissioners, I extend my sincere gratitude to the entire Commission staff for their dedication and commitment. I also wish to thank the many people who participated in our symposiums for their valuable contributions, as well as the members of the research and practitioners' advisory groups whose counsel significantly aided our undertaking.

Pierre Lortie
Chairman

INTRODUCTION

THE ROYAL COMMISSION'S research program constituted a comprehensive and detailed examination of the Canadian electoral process. The scope of the research, undertaken to assist Commissioners in their deliberations, was dictated by the broad mandate given to the Commission.

The objective of the research program was to provide Commissioners with a full account of the factors that have shaped our electoral democracy. This dictated, first and foremost, a focus on federal electoral law, but our inquiries also extended to the Canadian constitution, including the institutions of parliamentary government, the practices of political parties, the mass media and nonpartisan political organizations, as well as the decision-making role of the courts with respect to the constitutional rights of citizens. Throughout, our research sought to introduce a historical perspective in order to place the contemporary experience within the Canadian political tradition.

We recognized that neither our consideration of the factors shaping Canadian electoral democracy nor our assessment of reform proposals would be as complete as necessary if we failed to examine the experiences of Canadian provinces and territories and of other democracies. Our research program thus emphasized comparative dimensions in relation to the major subjects of inquiry.

Our research program involved, in addition to the work of the Commission's research coordinators, analysts and support staff, over 200 specialists from 28 universities in Canada, from the private sector and, in a number of cases, from abroad. Specialists in political science constituted the majority of our researchers, but specialists in law, economics, management, computer sciences, ethics, sociology and communications, among other disciplines, were also involved.

In addition to the preparation of research studies for the Commission, our research program included a series of research seminars, symposiums and workshops. These meetings brought together the Commissioners, researchers, representatives from the political parties, media personnel and others with practical experience in political parties, electoral politics and public affairs. These meetings provided not only a forum for discussion of the various subjects of the Commission's mandate, but also an opportunity for our research to be assessed by those with an intimate knowledge of the world of political practice.

These public reviews of our research were complemented by internal and external assessments of each research report by persons qualified in the area; such assessments were completed prior to our decision to publish any study in the series of research volumes.

The Research Branch of the Commission was divided into several areas, with the individual research projects in each area assigned to the research coordinators as follows:

F. Leslie Seidle	Political Party and Election Finance
Herman Bakvis	Political Parties
Kathy Megyery	Women, Ethno-Cultural Groups and Youth
David Small	Redistribution; Electoral Boundaries; Voter Registration
Janet Hiebert	Party Ethics
Michael Cassidy	Democratic Rights; Election Administration
Robert A. Milen	Aboriginal Electoral Participation and Representation
Frederick J. Fletcher	Mass Media and Broadcasting in Elections
David Mac Donald (Assistant Research Coordinator)	Direct Democracy

These coordinators identified appropriate specialists to undertake research, managed the projects and prepared them for publication. They also organized the seminars, symposiums and workshops in their research areas and were responsible for preparing presentations and briefings to help the Commission in its deliberations and decision making. Finally, they participated in drafting the Final Report of the Commission.

On behalf of the Commission, I welcome the opportunity to thank the following for their generous assistance in producing these research studies – a project that required the talents of many individuals.

In performing their duties, the research coordinators made a notable contribution to the work of the Commission. Despite the pressures of tight deadlines, they worked with unfailing good humour and the utmost congeniality. I thank all of them for their consistent support and cooperation.

In particular, I wish to express my gratitude to Leslie Seidle, senior research coordinator, who supervised our research analysts and support staff in Ottawa. His diligence, commitment and professionalism not only set high standards, but also proved contagious. I am grateful to Kathy Megyery, who performed a similar function in Montreal with equal aplomb and skill. Her enthusiasm and dedication inspired us all.

On behalf of the research coordinators and myself, I wish to thank our research analysts: Daniel Arsenault, Eric Bertram, Cécile Boucher, Peter Constantinou, Yves Denoncourt, David Docherty, Luc Dumont, Jane Dunlop, Scott Evans, Véronique Garneau, Keith Heintzman, Paul Holmes, Hugh Mellon, Cheryl D. Mitchell, Donald Padget, Alain Pelletier, Dominique Tremblay and Lisa Young. The Research Branch was strengthened by their ability to carry out research in a wide variety of areas, their intellectual curiosity and their team spirit.

The work of the research coordinators and analysts was greatly facilitated by the professional skills and invaluable cooperation of Research Branch staff members: Paulette LeBlanc, who, as administrative assistant, managed the flow of research projects; Hélène Leroux, secretary to the research coordinators, who produced briefing material for the Commissioners and who, with Lori Nazar, assumed responsibility for monitoring the progress of research projects in the latter stages of our work; Kathleen McBride and her assistant Natalie Brose, who created and maintained the database of briefs and hearings transcripts; and Richard Herold and his assistant Susan Dancause, who were responsible for our research library. Jacinthe Séguin and Cathy Tucker also deserve thanks – in addition to their duties as receptionists, they assisted in a variety of ways to help us meet deadlines.

We were extremely fortunate to obtain the research services of first-class specialists from the academic and private sectors. Their contributions are found in this and the other 22 published research volumes. We thank them for the quality of their work and for their willingness to contribute and to meet our tight deadlines.

Our research program also benefited from the counsel of Jean-Marc Hamel, Special Adviser to the Chairman of the Commission and former

Chief Electoral Officer of Canada, whose knowledge and experience proved invaluable.

In addition, numerous specialists assessed our research studies. Their assessments not only improved the quality of our published studies, but also provided us with much-needed advice on many issues. In particular, we wish to single out professors Donald Blake, Janine Brodie, Alan Cairns, Kenneth Carty, John Courtney, Peter Desbarats, Jane Jenson, Richard Johnston, Vincent Lemieux, Terry Morley and Joseph Wearing, as well as Ms. Beth Symes.

Producing such a large number of studies in less than a year requires a mastery of the skills and logistics of publishing. We were fortunate to be able to count on the Commission's Director of Communications, Richard Rochefort, and Assistant Director, Hélène Papineau. They were ably supported by the Communications staff: Patricia Burden, Louise Dagenais, Caroline Field, Claudine Labelle, France Langlois, Lorraine Maheux, Ruth McVeigh, Chantal Morissette, Sylvie Patry, Jacques Poitras and Claudette Rouleau-O'Toole.

To bring the project to fruition, the Commission also called on specialized contractors. We are deeply grateful for the services of Ann McCoomb (references and fact checking); Marthe Lemery, Pierre Chagnon and the staff of Communications Com'ça (French quality control); Norman Bloom, Pamela Riseborough and associates of B&B Editorial Consulting (English adaptation and quality control); and Mado Reid (French production). Al Albania and his staff at Acart Graphics designed the studies and produced some 2 400 tables and figures.

The Commission's research reports constitute Canada's largest publishing project of 1991. Successful completion of the project required close cooperation between the public and private sectors. In the public sector, we especially acknowledge the excellent service of the Privy Council unit of the Translation Bureau, Department of the Secretary of State of Canada, under the direction of Michel Parent, and our contacts Ruth Steele and Terry Denovan of the Canada Communication Group, Department of Supply and Services.

The Commission's co-publisher for the research studies was Dundurn Press of Toronto, whose exceptional service is gratefully acknowledged. Wilson & Lafleur of Montreal, working with the Centre de Documentation Juridique du Québec, did equally admirable work in preparing the French version of the studies.

Teams of editors, copy editors and proofreaders worked diligently under stringent deadlines with the Commission and the publishers to prepare some 20 000 pages of manuscript for design, typesetting and printing. The work of these individuals, whose names are listed elsewhere in this volume, was greatly appreciated.

Our acknowledgements extend to the contributions of the Commission's Executive Director, Guy Goulard, and the administration and executive support teams: Maurice Lacasse, Denis Lafrance and Steve Tremblay (finance); Thérèse Lacasse and Mary Guy-Shea (personnel); Cécile Desforges (assistant to the Executive Director); Marie Dionne (administration); Anna Bevilacqua (records); and support staff members Michelle Bélanger, Roch Langlois, Michel Lauzon, Jean Mathieu, David McKay and Pierrette McMurtie, as well as Denise Miquelon and Christiane Séguin of the Montreal office.

A special debt of gratitude is owed to Marlène Girard, assistant to the Chairman. Her ability to supervise the logistics of the Commission's work amid the tight schedules of the Chairman and Commissioners contributed greatly to the completion of our task.

I also wish to express my deep gratitude to my own secretary, Liette Simard. Her superb administrative skills and great patience brought much-appreciated order to my penchant for the chaotic workstyle of academe. She also assumed responsibility for the administrative coordination of revisions to the final drafts of volumes 1 and 2 of the Commission's Final Report. I owe much to her efforts and assistance.

Finally, on behalf of the research coordinators and myself, I wish to thank the Chairman, Pierre Lortie, the members of the Commission, Pierre Fortier, Robert Gabor, William Knight and Lucie Pépin, and former members Elwood Cowley and Senator Donald Oliver. We are honoured to have worked with such an eminent and thoughtful group of Canadians, and we have benefited immensely from their knowledge and experience. In particular, we wish to acknowledge the creativity, intellectual rigour and energy our Chairman brought to our task. His unparalleled capacity to challenge, to bring out the best in us, was indeed inspiring.

Peter Aucoin
Director of Research

PREFACE

ALTHOUGH WOMEN WERE granted the vote and the right to candidacy some 60 years ago, by 1988 they had achieved only 13 percent representation in the House of Commons. This persistent and significant under-representation has consequences that are more than symbolic; it deprives our federal policy-making process of the input of a significant number of Canadians on the nature and timing of public policy issues. This is not to suggest that women hold homogeneous views on all public policy issues, or that they do not respond along partisan lines on many others. Nonetheless, a system that does not, over time, come closer to adequately representing its citizenship calls into question the legitimacy of its democratic institutions.

What are the reasons behind this poor showing of women in political parties and in federal office? Five studies were commissioned to address this specific issue. Although the focus of their investigations differed, the similarity of the conclusions and prescriptions for reform reached by the authors of this volume is striking. Their discussions and conclusions helped to inform the Commission's recommendations.

Janine Brodie provides a broad overview of the role and performance of women in federal politics. She underscores that during the last 20 years the percentage of women candidates and MPs has risen markedly – from 6 percent in 1972 to 19 percent in 1988 for female candidates; from 2 percent in 1972 to 13 percent in 1988 for women MPs. She attributes these gains to changing perceptions of the role of women in society and the efforts of feminists both inside and outside party organizations to increase the representation of women in Canadian politics. She emphasizes, however, that this progress remains marginal and that it should not be assumed that these gains are inevitable, permanent or sufficient.

According to Brodie, the major barriers to women's entry into the political system include the cost of contesting party nominations and the tendency among political parties to place women in marginal ridings. She concludes that, in and of itself, the removal of legal barriers to women's participation will not lead to gender parity. Specific actions to compensate for women's historical disadvantage are required.

Sylvia Bashevkin analyses the participation of women in political parties by assessing their presence and their role at different levels of the political hierarchy. Her findings confirm previous research: As positions in politics become more competitive and more powerful, the number of women occupying them declines. Specifically, she notes that at the local level women are still much less likely to hold decision-making positions in riding associations than to fill clerical positions. At the intermediate level of political involvement, such as party executive member or campaign manager, women are increasingly active, yet they still occupy only a minority of these positions. At the candidacy level, women are severely under-represented. She describes how this under-representation has prompted pressure from interest groups, political action groups and feminist groups to reform the system. According to Bashevkin, political parties should increase female representation in the Canadian political process, since voters clearly accept women as equal participants in that process.

Lynda Erickson examines the impact of the candidate selection process on the composition of the House of Commons, identifying the Canadian nomination system as one of the key barriers to achieving greater gender parity. Although some measures have been taken by Canadian political parties in the past decade, they have not translated into significant increases in the number of women candidates and MPs. Erickson focuses on party selection procedures to assess their impact on the number of women being nominated in ridings where they have a chance of winning. She then considers various proposals for increasing the number of women in competitive party candidacies. Her proposals for reform include limiting expenditures at the nomination phase, providing centralized funding for nomination contests and changing the nature of political life in Canada to make it more hospitable to women.

One factor frequently cited as a barrier to the election of women in the United States, most notably to Congress, is the low rate of legislative turnover. In her study, Lisa Young examines whether this proposition applies to the Canadian situation. Based on a simulation of legislative turnover, she concludes that Canada's relatively high rate of turnover in the House of Commons constitutes an opportunity for women seeking access to federal office and that other factors are clearly the cause of the under-representation of women as candidates and MPs. She suggests that, as the gatekeepers of the political process, political parties alter their recruitment and nomination practices if a substantial change in the number of women MPs is to be achieved.

Gertrude Robinson and Armande Saint-Jean focus on the impact of media coverage on women politicians and trace the evolution of stereotypes that have been applied to women politicians over the past 30 years. They find that women politicians receive, on balance, less coverage than their male counterparts and that the coverage they do receive is tainted by stereotyping news values that tend to emphasize family relations and physical attractiveness, aspects rarely referred to in the coverage of male politicians. They conclude that, while a more gender-neutral style of reporting is developing, women politicians are still subjected to different media treatment and standards of behaviour. They conclude that as active participants in social change, the media have a crucial role to play in shaping the progress and legitimacy of women's access to political life.

I would like to thank the Commissioners for their persistence in addressing this issue and Peter Aucoin, Director of Research, for his unfailing and cheerful support.

Kathy Megyery
Research Coordinator

WOMEN IN
CANADIAN
POLITICS

1

WOMEN AND THE ELECTORAL PROCESS IN CANADA

Janine Brodie
with the assistance of
Celia Chandler

OVERVIEW

POPULAR DEMOCRATIC IDEOLOGY provides that every citizen has the right to participate in the process of democratic decision making and to seek public office. In practice, however, many social interests are not represented in the policy-making process. Only a small proportion of the population seeks elected office and even fewer are elected. Although all enfranchised voters have the same legal right to contest democratic election, subtle structural, social and political practices narrow the field of potential political leaders to a select few.

The Under-representation of Women
Among the social groups most consistently excluded from the ranks of the political élite are the poor, minority ethnic and religious groups and women. Statistics indicate, however, that women are the most under-represented social group in the elected assemblies of the world (Putnam 1976, 32). Women everywhere constitute more than one-half of the population and, at the same time, rarely are more than a handful of the political élite. Few aspects of social life are more male-dominated than electoral politics. Although in recent decades women have entered non-traditional occupations with increasing frequency, legislative office remains an elusive goal for the vast majority of Canadian women.

The issue of women's political representation has occupied the political agenda of Western democracies, with varying degrees of intensity, for most of the 20th century. At the turn of the century, the first wave of the women's movement fought to secure for women formal equality with men with respect to citizenship rights. The extension of the franchise, however, failed to open the doors of political power to women. Indeed, as the Royal Commission on the Status of Women (RCSW) reported in 1970, women constituted less than 1 percent of those elected in all the federal and provincial elections in the 50 years after women's enfranchisement. The Commission concluded that women had only achieved "a token recognition" of their right to be represented in Parliament. Legislating the means and goals of Canada's social, economic and political development continued to be an exclusive male prerogative (Canada, Royal Commission 1970, 339, 355).

In the years since the release of the RCSW report, Canada has witnessed the growth of a new round of mobilization around the unfinished agenda of gender equality. Second-wave feminism has motivated major attitudinal and behavioural changes among individual Canadians and, at the level of formal politics, has mounted a concerted challenge to the barriers that continue to restrict the achievement of gender equality in all walks of Canadian life, including electoral politics. Considering the minimal progress of women in legislative politics in the first 50 years after suffrage, the growth in women's participation in federal elections

Table 1.1
Women candidates and MPs in Canadian general elections
(percent of total)

Year elected	Candidates	Elected
1921–67	2.4	0.8
1968	3.5	0.4
1972	6.4	1.8
1974	9.4	3.4
1979	13.8	3.6
1980	14.4	5.0
1984	14.5	9.6
1988	19.2	13.4

Source: Elections Canada.

in the past 20 years has been significant. Women, as a percentage of federal candidates, have increased from 6 percent in 1972 to 19 percent in 1988. During the same period, women increased their representation in the House of Commons from 2 percent to 13 percent (see table 1.1).

The Uncertain Watershed

According to many political analysts, the representational gains of the past decade signal the long-awaited watershed for women in Canadian politics. Beginning with the 1984 federal election, each of the major political parties scrambled to nominate a record number of women candidates, and for the first time in Canadian election history, the three major party leaders participated in a nationally televised debate that was devoted exclusively to political issues of special concern to women. In that year, 27 women were elected to the House of Commons – nearly double the record set in 1980 – and six women were appointed to the

Figure 1.1
Number of women elected to the House of Commons by year

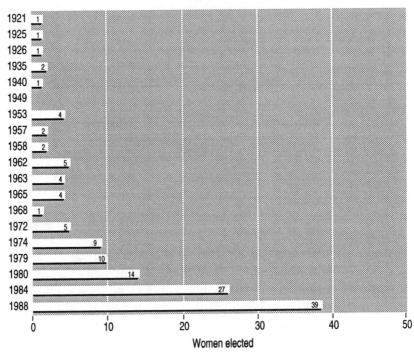

Source: Elections Canada.

Table 1.2
Women's representation in the provinces
(percentages, most recent election)

Province	Women in legislature	Women candidates
British Columbia	13.0	21.0
Alberta	15.0	18.0
Saskatchewan	8.0	25.0
Manitoba	18.0	21.0
Ontario	22.0	23.0
Quebec	22.0	18.0
New Brunswick	12.0	16.0
Nova Scotia	6.0	21.0
Prince Edward Island	22.0	25.0
Newfoundland	2.0	8.0
Northwest Territories	8.0	—
Yukon	31.0	—

Source: Royal Commission on Electoral Reform and Party Financing.

federal cabinet, again twice the previous record. Women continued to make impressive representational gains later in the decade. The 1988 federal election brought 39 women to Parliament (Gotell and Brodie 1991). Women's representation in provincial legislatures and territorial assemblies reflects a similar upward trend (see figure 1.1). Currently, women hold approximately 15 percent of provincial and territorial seats. In three provinces, they make up more than 20 percent of the elected assembly (see table 1.2).

It is both premature and ill-advised, however, to suggest that these marginal gains represent the beginning of an inevitable or natural progression toward gender parity in our elected institutions. These gains reflect the changing orientations of the Canadian public toward women's role in society and the concerted efforts of feminists, both inside and outside party organizations, to increase the representation of women in Canadian politics. As a result of this pressure and increased public awareness, Canadian political parties can no longer afford to offer a slate of candidates that includes no or very few women. Nevertheless, statistical analysis suggests that women candidates still are not afforded the same opportunities for election as their male counterparts. Although

Table 1.3
Success rates among female and male candidates, 1972–88
(percentages)

Year	Women elected	Men elected
1972	7.6	25.6
1974	7.2	20.4
1979	5.1	22.1
1980	6.4	20.0
1984	12.8	20.6
1988	12.9	20.1

Source: Elections Canada.

improving, the success rates of women candidates in federal elections are still approximately one-half that of men (see table 1.3).

Women candidates are less often elected, partly because they often choose to run for a minor party. More importantly, however, the major federal parties continue to follow the long-established tradition of nominating women to ridings where their chances of winning are low. Indeed, many of the representational gains that women have achieved over the past decade occurred precisely when their party was not expected to win at the beginning of the campaign. Women were nominated to ridings that, at the time the writ was issued, seemed hopeless, but were elected to office because of the volatility characteristic of the electorate in the 1980s and unexpected shifts in voter support for their party during the campaign. The 1984 federal and 1990 Ontario elections are cases in point. Any optimism about the inevitability of women's representational gains should be tempered with a hard dose of political reality. Nominating women to seemingly lost-cause ridings and waiting for electoral volatility and an unexpected electoral tide to sweep them into office is hardly a promising strategy for increasing the political representation of women in Canada.

Changes in the conduct of Canadian election campaigns also caution against a laissez-faire posture toward the election of women. Over the course of the last decade, federal elections have been characterized by dramatic increases in the cost of contesting a party nomination and in pre-writ election spending. Neither of these campaign expenditures are regulated by federal legislation, yet both severely disadvantage women who, on average, have less access to financial resources than men. Women may be more prepared to offer themselves as candidates for public office than in the past, but financial constraints, unless controlled, will increasingly and effectively bar them from effective competition in the future. Increases in campaign expenditures threaten the potential gains in political representation of all groups that sit disproportionately at the bottom of the socio-economic hierarchy.

Evidence drawn from the international experience also indicates that there is nothing natural or automatic about increasing the election of women. The Inter-Parliamentary Union, for example, reported that the percentage of women among the world's legislators has dropped over the past year and has remained "strikingly stagnant" for the past 15 years. In July 1989, women constituted 12.7 percent of the world's representative assemblies compared to 12.5 percent in 1975 (*Globe and Mail* 1989, A12).

Canada's record of electing women to national office ranks at approximately the mid-point of established liberal democracies. During the 1980s, Canada surpassed the record of the United States, the United Kingdom, Australia and France. Yet, the election of women in Canada

Table 1.4
Women's political representation internationally (Lower House)

Country	Women members (%)	Year
Canada	13.4	1988
Australia	6.1	1987
Belgium	7.5	1986
United Kingdom	6.3	1987
United States	5.7	1988
Sweden	28.9	1986
Switzerland	10.2	1986
Norway	34.9	1987
Finland	30.5	1986
Denmark	25.7	1986
West Germany	15.0	1987
France	4.4	1986
New Zealand	14.4	1987

Sources: Canadian Advisory Council on the Status of Women (1987, 17); Hill and Roberts (1990).

still does not reach the levels set in Sweden, Norway and Finland – countries that have made concerted efforts to increase the election of women and have proportional-representation electoral systems (see table 1.4).

Although Canada has made marginal progress toward gender parity, we should not assume that these gains are inevitable, permanent or sufficient. Canada's legislatures continue to be a poor mirror of the population. The voice of government, as the Royal Commission on the Status of Women observed 20 years ago, is still a man's voice. Women remain governed rather than governors, legislated rather than legislators. Without representation, economic, political and social decisions are taken with little attention given to, or even awareness of, the special impact that new policy initiatives have on women.

The persistent under-representation of women in Canadian politics raises fundamental questions about both the legitimacy of our democratic institutions and the biases of electoral politics. Few doubt that this under-representation is directly related to women's subordinate status in society as a whole. Although diminishing somewhat, Canadian society is characterized by a gendered division of labour in which women are not valued as much as men are. Occupations that are characterized as "women's work" pay much less than those that are typically considered "male." Men continue to be paid more and have greater opportunities for advancement than women who perform the same work, much less work of equal value.

By all indicators women are a subordinate group in Canadian society, and as for any subordinate group, the issue of political representation poses a seemingly unresolvable dilemma. Politics and political representation are critical for the socially disadvantaged. Through the political process, their interests are translated into political demands, which are placed on the legislative agenda and advanced through legislation. The process of liberal-democratic recruitment, left unregulated, however, tends to favour the representation of the socially advantaged. The less powerful need politics to redress their inequality, but their inequality prevents them from achieving any significant measure of political power. Social and political inequalities, in other words, tend to reinforce one another in liberal democracies, forming a system of inclusion and exclusion.

This study provides an overview of the most recent research concerning women's interrelationship with electoral politics. It is divided into four parts beginning with the gendered nature of liberal democracy itself. It continues to examine women's political participation in the electorate, in political parties and as candidates for federal office. The study concludes that formal equality – that is, the removal of legal barriers to women's participation in political life – has not and will not lead to gender parity in political representation. More is required to compensate for women's historical disadvantage in liberal democratic politics (Clark 1988, 271). Recommendations to achieve this goal are provided in the conclusion.

WOMEN AND LIBERAL DEMOCRACY

Explaining Women's Exclusion

Until recently, political science and society in general did not question why, in a liberal democracy, the nominal majority was virtually excluded from exercising political power. Male dominance in politics was either assumed to be natural and, therefore, not subject to academic investigation or political mobilization, or it was explained away by pointing to the alleged incapacities of women to compete effectively with men for public office.

Numerous explanations have been offered for why women have failed to achieve political office. The macro-historical perspective, for example, proposes that the equal integration of women into democratic decision-making structures (like the integration of all newly enfranchised groups) follows two distinct and necessarily consecutive stages. First, the voting participation of newly enfranchised groups must rise until it matches that of already established groups in the electorate. Only after the first stage has been accomplished can we expect to find representatives of these late entrants participating in élite politics. According to this explanation, then, the political representation of women is contingent upon women voting in the same numbers as men – the "established" group in the electorate.

Other explanations focus on the supposed incapacities of women to compete in electoral politics. The "socialization" explanation, for example, contends that women do not seek elected office because women are socialized to be apolitical. Women do not exercise political power because they don't wish to. In a similar vein, "gender-role" or "situational" explanations contend that women do not abstain from politics as much as they are inhibited from doing so by the constraints of traditional gender roles, especially motherhood (Brodie 1985, chap. 1).

Female Deficiencies

While each of these strains of argument finds some support in the literature, there are two sets of assumptions underlying these arguments that should be questioned. First, and most fundamentally, the under-representation of women is explained in terms of a female deficiency. Women are not up to par with men in terms of participation, interests or life experience and, therefore, do not achieve elected office. The extension of this argument is that women must be like men if they expect to gain representation. It is assumed that women's difference from men cannot be integrated into or represented within the corridors of power. Instead, their difference explains their exclusion from power. In other words, the norms of politics, although narrowly defined and posed in gender neutral terms, are, in fact, male norms to which women are expected to conform if they are to achieve power. Put even more bluntly, these explanations propose that women, and not the electoral system, must change if gender parity is to be achieved.

The seemingly immutable nature of the electoral system is the central thread underlying the second set of assumptions in these explanations. In brief, it is assumed that the process of democratic elections is gender neutral and divorced from history. It is depicted as a set of rules or procedures that stands independently from the gendered division of labour and is blind to the gender of its participants. Yet, these assumptions pale against the history of liberal democracies. The very meaning of democracy has been subject to continuous challenge, and the practice of democratic elections has been subject to ongoing change. Our understanding of democracy and democratic procedure does not exist as an abstract, pure form but, rather, is the product of historical change, political mobilization, and ultimately, public policy. Put differently, the rules for conducting democratic elections are not simply a neutral terrain upon which politics is played out. They are frequently the object of political struggle itself.

These conflicting views of elections, either as immutable or historically contingent, are not without important political ramifications. The former conflates the meaning of democracy with a historically frozen set of rules and demands that the population conform to the rules or risk exclusion and alienation from formal political institutions. It makes no allowance for new social forces that have fewer resources or less experience to play by the established rules of the game, and it discounts the democratic goal of adapting the system to respond to the changing demands and needs of the polity. The historical perspective, in contrast, views existing democratic procedures as variable and manipulable, and a means of responding to society's changing political needs and understanding of democracy. It treats electoral procedures as the product of political moments, the object of public policy and a reflection of a society's understanding of the meaning of democracy.

The Origins of Liberal Democracy

Although casting a vote as a method of democratic decision making can be traced back to the *polis* of ancient Greece, democratic elections as they are now popularly understood are relatively recent in the evolution of governing instruments. For the ancient Greeks, democracy simply meant rule by citizens. Neither slavery nor the exclusion of the majority of the population, including women, from participating in these nascent democracies was considered problematical because it was understood that the rules applied only to citizens. According to this notion of democracy, nature had ordained that all people were not equal and that citizenship extended only to a select group of males (Clark 1988, 264).

The origins of the modern democratic election, complete with its conception of formal political equality, are relatively recent and inseparably linked to the unfolding relationship between capitalism and the liberal democratic form of government. Most liberal democracies came into being in two distinct phases: first they were liberal, and then, much later, popular democratic institutions and procedures followed. Canada's particular system of parliamentary democracy is modelled on that of the British. There, merchants and industrialists seeking freedom from the feudal order were the major social force behind liberalism's important innovations in social organization and political thinking such as free enterprise, individualism, formal political rights and responsible government (Brodie and Jenson 1989, chap. 1).

Throughout most Western countries, liberal democratic institutions gradually replaced monarchical forms of rule. This fundamental change in institutional form, however, was achieved only after intense – often revolutionary – political conflict between the rising bourgeoisie and elements of the old order. It was also based on a very narrow definition of democratic equality. The franchise was restricted to men of property.[1] Although these early liberal democratic regimes were founded on the principle that all men were equal, some men were clearly more equal than others. Universal male suffrage, regular elections and guarantees of freedom of speech and association were achieved only after protracted and bitter confrontations between the politically powerful (whose social base was in the capitalist class) and the growing working class of industrial capitalism.

The Woman Question

As a political ideology, liberalism pronounced a new politics based on the values of individualism, formal political equality and equality of opportunity. These values continue to predominate in Western societies. Nevertheless, from the outset, they were not assumed to apply to women. Early liberal theorists argued that the fundamental equality among citizens stemmed either from the state of nature or the social contract (Clark 1988, 267). Liberal individualism, however, denied that women could be citizens. Hobbes, for example, recommended that the family should be represented in the political sphere by only one person – the husband, who could interpret and act for the political interests of its members. Locke, by contrast, argued that women voluntarily relinquished their political sovereignty when they entered into a marriage contract, which legitimately subjugated the wife's will to that of her husband.

While it is often assumed that the early liberal theorists simply overlooked the "woman question," this assumption finds little support in the historical record. Liberalism was, in fact, "enacted on the field of gender" (Scott 1986, 1069). The issue of women's political status and rights, especially their exclusion from the emerging liberal political order, was of critical importance to the classical theorists. And, with few exceptions, they concluded that women should not be extended citizenship rights. They relied on biological determinism or women's segregation and subordination in the domestic sphere to conclude that women were permanently impaired from developing the requisite skills for democratic citizenship (Jones 1988, 11, 15). Thus, women were barred by law from participating in liberal democratic politics and institutions.

Liberalism represented a revolutionary transformation of the social and political world, which, as Walzer correctly emphasizes, was based on the art of separation. Feudal society was fractured into a series of different realms, each governed by its own rules and procedures. The church was separated from the state. The former was governed by theocracy and the latter by liberal democracy. Similarly, the political and economic spheres were separated so that a free market could develop according to the rules of capitalism, free from state interference. The state also was, in varying degrees, separated from the monarchy, opening both the government and the bureaucracy to the rules of political competition and meritocracy. Finally, a line was drawn between public and private life. The realm of the private, of personal and family life, was sacred ground upon which the state could not tread (Walzer 1984).

Of course, as numerous critics of liberal democracy argue, the lines of separation between church and state, politics and economics, and public and private were never complete. Indeed, with the evolution of universal male suffrage and mass elections, it became readily apparent that the formal political equality guaranteed to men in the political sphere meant very little when held against the substantive inequalities characteristic of the economic sphere. Economic élites could, and regularly did, convert their economic resources into political capital, thereby subverting the fundamental premises of formal political equality and democratic elections. A brief survey of the history of legislation regulating democratic elections reveals a litany of attempts to contain the impact of market forces on the democratic process. The introduction of the secret ballot, restrictions on vote buying and other corrupt practices, liquor laws, and electoral financing legislation all attempt to contain the power of money in the electoral process. Put differently, liberal democratic governments everywhere have consistently recognized that the substantive inequalities emanating from only *one* of liberalism's social divisions – the division between economics and politics – had to be regulated to maintain a semblance of integrity in the democratic process.

The Public–Private Divide

In many ways, however, liberalism's division between the public and private spheres has had a more pervasive and enduring effect on electoral politics, both in terms of establishing the legislative agenda of liberal democracies and selecting who would do the representing. It institutionalized a gendered division of labour and placed men and women in different worlds. Even though many poor women were in the labour force, the public–private split deemed that the public world of politics and economics was the proper sphere for males and the private world of the home and family was the proper sphere for females. Women were relegated to the private sphere by biological fiat that, in turn, was reformulated with the institutionalization of the public and private domains at the political level (Eisenstein 1981, 14).

The public and private spheres, like the church and the state or politics and economics, were governed by different rules. The public sphere was defined by the rules of liberal democracy and the norms of universalism, equality and reason while the private sphere was a world of inequality, subjection and emotion (Siim 1988, 163). It was simply assumed that women were subject to the rule of the man "in his castle" – a place where the state dared not tread. Liberal democracy, therefore, as Pateman (1985, 192) rightly contends, has built into itself a contradiction between the ideals of individual freedom and equality in the public sphere and the assumption that women are naturally subject to men in the family. Women's dependence and obedience in turn made them unsuitable candidates for democratic citizenship rights (Clark 1988, 274). Although our understanding of what constitutes the public and private has changed dramatically since the early days of liberal democracy, belief in these separate spheres is still central to the way we think about liberal democracy and how we actually structure our lives (Burt 1986, 114).

The gendered foundations of liberal democracy had, and continue to have, profound implications for women in politics. It meant that women were denied the most basic political rights such as voting and running for political office until relatively recently. The extension of the franchise, however, did not overcome the liabilities of the public–private divide for women. Popular ideology and practical experience continue to reinforce the notion that politics is a more appropriate "masculine" than "feminine" activity and that all women embody personality traits that are inappropriate for the public sphere. Moreover, even if women challenge this pervasive cultural prohibition, few have the resources to compete with men in the political arena. As one analyst has observed, women's power in the home is like soft currency in the international market: it is not convertible in the public sphere (Jonasdottir 1988, 46).

Of course, most Canadian women are no longer solely confined to the private sphere. They combine their domestic roles with participation in the paid labour market. Economic life, however, is similarly characterized by a gendered division of labour. Most women are concentrated in low-wage sectors performing manual, support or "nurturing" roles – tasks deemed suitable for the "feminine" character. Few women are employed in jobs that produce "social capital," the social knowledge, contacts and privileged access to culturally valued qualifications and social skills (Lovenduski 1986, 209). Few have the personal financial security or access to moneyed networks, which are increasingly necessary to launch a successful career in politics.

Liberalism's public–private split has put women in a historical and structural disadvantage in relation to electoral politics. Equally important, this division tends to exclude so-called women's issues from the political sphere and render their political interests invisible. Liberalism is founded on the assumption that the public is fundamentally distinct from the private and personal (Jones 1988, 12). This constitutes a structural barrier that filters issues out of the public agenda. Issues relating to the family, the gendered division of labour, child care, reproduction, sexuality and others generally have not been considered political and, therefore, amenable to public policy solutions; sometimes they are simply treated as trivial "women's issues" that can be easily demoted down the rank of legislative priorities. This substantive division-exclusion, in turn, generates an understanding among many women that politics is irrelevant to a large part of their lives. They may demonstrate less interest in legislative politics than men because it does not address their interests or speak to their experience.

WOMEN IN THE CANADIAN ELECTORATE

Gender and the Electorate

In the postwar years, the weight of research on women in electoral politics has concentrated on the behaviour of women in the electorate. This focus partly reflects trends in the discipline of political science as well as the simple fact that there were so few women in political office to study. More importantly, however, political scientists tended to view gender differences in the electorate as explanations for why women were vastly under-represented in élite political roles within political parties and in elected assemblies. Both the macro-historical and micro theories of the sociology of political participation posit a causal link between mass political behaviour and élite recruitment (see Brodie 1985, chap. 1). The macro-historical perspective, as discussed above, is concerned with the integration of newly enfranchised groups into the mainstream of democratic politics. It asserts that the necessary precondition for the recruitment of women to public office is that women vote in the same numbers as men – the already established group in the electorate (see Means 1976, 382–83).

Lester Milbrath's hierarchy of political involvement best illustrates the link that is drawn between mass political behaviour and élite recruitment in micro theories of political participation. Milbrath (1965, chap. 1) argues that the citizens of any democratic polity can be ranked on a ladder of political activities. The ladder has four distinct and hierarchically ordered steps. At the bottom of this hierarchy are "Apathetics," who neither care about politics nor vote. "Spectators" are placed a step above the former group because they take some interest in politics and engage in the least demanding acts of democratic citizenship such as voting or putting a campaign sign on their lawn. "Transitional" participants are on the next step up the ladder of political involvement. They may attend political meetings, contact public officials or contribute financially to a party. At the top are the "Gladiators" – party activists, strategists, fund-raisers and candidates.[2]

This model assumes that political participation is cumulative. By making this assumption, Milbrath establishes a link between mass participation and office-holding. In terms of his model, "cumulative" means that those at any one level on the ladder also perform the political acts that define the lower levels. Spectator activity is a prerequisite for transitional activity, which, in turn, is a precondition for gladiatorial roles.

The transitional level, in other words, provides the "pool of eligibles" for public office. The existence of biases in liberal-democratic recruitment, therefore, simply reflects the underparticipation of certain social groups at lower levels of the hierarchy of political involvement – especially the composition of the "pool" from which full-time politicians emerge.

Both the macro and micro explanations rely on similar evidence to explain the gender biases in political representation. Both focus on gender differences in rates of mass political behaviour, and both assume that the election of women is dependent on the development of parity between the sexes in mass political participation. Early voting studies reported that women were less likely to vote than men. This finding was repeatedly taken as evidence that women had not yet achieved the first and necessary stage in the political integration of "late entrants" into the political life of liberal democracies. Similarly, early political participation studies indicated that women were less likely to move up the ladder of political involvement to the transitional level. From the micro perspective, too, gender biases in political representation could be attributed to the seeming inability of women in the electorate to enter the ranks of the eligibles for public office at rates similar to men.

Both explanations for male dominance at the élite level tend to blame the "victims" for their lack of political power. Neither model includes in its conceptualization the idea that women might face structural impediments in their quest for political representation or that the system might be gender-biased. More importantly, however, these conclusions were grounded on the flimsiest of empirical evidence. The smallest of gender differences in voter turnout were taken as an explanation for women's exclusion from the corridors of power. It was only after women political scientists began to re-examine the data that this kind of explanation was challenged either as outdated or as gender-biased in its conception. Study after study demonstrated that, at the citizen level, women did participate at levels comparable to men's, especially when relevant socio-demographic factors were controlled (Chandler 1990; Evans 1980; Randall 1987).

Voter Turnout

Certainly, the gender differences in voter turnout in Canadian federal elections hardly seem sufficient to account for the virtual exclusion of women from the House of Commons. Indeed, evidence taken from Canadian National Election Studies (CNES) in the period between 1965 and 1988 indicates that only once in the past seven federal elections was there a statistically significant gender difference in voter turnout

Table 1.5
Voter turnout by sex, 1965–88 Canadian National Election Studies

Year	N	Men voting (%)	Women voting (%)
1965	1 983	86.8	83.9
1968	2 767	86.8	84.2
1974	2 461	86.5	83.9
1979	2 697	90.2	88.5
1980	1 747	88.8	86.6
1984*	3 375	87.4	84.2
1988	2 919	87.2	89.0

Source: Chandler (1990).

*Chi-square significant at .01 level.

(see table 1.5). Results from the CNES indicate that 87 percent of men compared with 84 percent of women voted in the 1984 federal election. There is no apparent reason for this statistically significant gender difference. It may, in fact, simply reflect sampling error. Regardless, a gender difference of approximately 3 percent in the electorate hardly seems sufficient to explain a 90 percent gender gap in the composition of the House of Commons after the 1984 campaign. Indeed, in 1988 women's turnout exceeded that of men, but the gender gap in representation was 87 percent.

Although gender differences in federal turnout have been minuscule in the past 25 years, other studies have shown that several demographic factors are related to levels of political participation among Canadian women. For example, John Terry (1984) found that employment outside the home and education were positively related to women's turnout. Black and McGlen's (1979) survey of federal elections between 1965 and 1974 also confirms the positive effects of labour-force participation on women's political participation. However, the latter study and Kay et al. (1988) indicate that the presence of children in the home constrains women's political participation regardless of whether child rearing is coupled with labour-force participation (see also Chandler 1990, 21).

In the past 25 years, gender differences in federal turnout have hovered around 2.5 percent. Nevertheless, one finds much larger differences in the orientations of women and men toward the political system during the same period. Table 1.6 shows the responses of men and women in the electorate in 1965 and 1984 to a number of items designed to test citizen orientations to the system. A few general observations can be made from these data. First, the gender gaps on these items were much wider in the 1960s than in the 1980s. Second, across this period both men and women indicate greater levels of alienation, believing, for example, that the government does not listen to them and that elected officials soon lose touch with their constituents. Nevertheless, some significant gender gaps in the orientations of men and women to the political system remain. In the 1980s as in the 1960s women are less likely than men to express an interest in politics and more likely to feel that politics is too complicated for them.

Table 1.6
Orientations toward electoral politics by sex and year
(percentages)

	National Election Studies			
	1965		1984	
	Women (N = 1 033)	Men (N = 1 075)	Women (N = 1 910)	Men (N = 1 467)
A. Interest in politics*				
A lot	20.2	31.4	15.5	22.5
Some	43.2	44.1	40.7	48.3
Not much	36.6	24.5	43.8	29.2
B. Trust in federal government				
Always	9.6	9.8	10.5	13.1
Mostly	51.7	51.0	52.5	50.0
Sometimes	38.7	39.2	37.0	37.0
C. Government doesn't care what people like me think				
Agree	52.0	47.0	65.7	64.0
Disagree	48.0	53.0	34.3	36.0
D. Politics is too complicated to understand				
Agree	79.5	64.7	71.8	60.5
Disagree	20.5	35.3	28.2	39.5
E. People like me don't have a say in politics				
Agree	55.1	48.8	64.8	64.0
Disagree	44.9	51.2	35.2	36.0
F. Elected MPs soon lose touch				
Agree	58.5	61.0	76.9	75.0
Disagree	41.6	39.0	23.1	25.0

Source: 1965 and 1984 Canadian National Election Studies.

*The variables in the 1984 study have been recoded to reflect the 1965 three-point ordinal scale.

The Gender Gap

During the past decade, academic investigations of women in the electorate have shifted to analyses of the so-called gender gap and the
effects of second-wave feminism on the orientations of the electorate.
The gender gap refers to evidence of women acting as a cohesive bloc
in the electorate and can take three different forms. First, women may
participate in electoral politics at significantly higher levels or in different
ways than their male counterparts. Second, women may assess key
political issues differently than men. Third, men and women may differ significantly in terms of party choice.

Traditionally, it was assumed that women and men in the electorate
responded in similar ways to issues and political parties. Indeed, the
failure of women to act as a cohesive political force after their enfranchisement resulted in many analysts assuming that women simply followed their husbands in electoral politics. The behaviour of women in
the electorate immediately after suffrage is a matter of conjecture because
public opinion data are not available for this period. Nevertheless, mass
surveys conducted in the 1950s, 1960s and 1970s showed little evidence
of women acting as a political bloc either in relation to political issues
or party choice. In Canada, for example, an article reviewing the attitudes of women and men toward a broad range of political issues over
the 1960–1978 period found few and only small gender differences in
issue orientation (Fletcher and Drummond 1979).

Beginning in the late 1970s, however, pollsters in many Western
democracies began to discern growing gender differences in both issue
orientation and party choice. Women finally appeared to be forming a
distinctive bloc in the electorate. In Great Britain, for example, pollsters
found that women were much less likely than men to support Margaret
Thatcher's Conservative party and its neo-conservative political agenda.
British women were much more concerned than men with preserving
welfare programs and increasing government spending in the areas of
education, health, social services and housing (Rogers 1983, 158). In
1980, an unexpectedly large gender gap emerged in the American presidential election. Pollsters found that 8 percent fewer women than
men voted for Ronald Reagan and that, for the first time since data
have been collected, more women than men voted (Mueller 1988, 16;
Chandler 1990, 4). Further analysis also showed that American women
were much less likely than men to support Reagan's neo-conservative
platform and his rejection of the Equal Rights Amendment (ERA). By the
1982 American mid-term elections, the gender gap had grown to the
extent that three gubernatorial losses were attributed to it (Mueller
1988, 29).

The emergence of a gender gap in the American electorate both encouraged the women's movement and threatened the reigning Republican regime. The organized women's movement, for its part, reviewed its assessment of electoral politics and geared its activity to sustaining and expanding the gap in the American electorate. In 1982, "The Women's Vote Project" was launched. Rallying under the slogan, "It's a man's world unless women vote," this organization set for itself the goal of registering 1.5 million new women voters for the 1984 presidential election. It actually exceeded its goal by 300 000 women voters (Mendelson 1988, 69, 75). As a result, women constituted 53.5 percent of voters in the 1984 election, a plurality of approximately 3 million voters (Mueller 1988, 22). In concert, the National Organization of Women (NOW) used the gender gap as a powerful strategic tool to pressure the Democratic party to nominate a woman vice-presidential candidate for the 1984 election (ibid., 29). NOW also raised more than $1.5 million in campaign funds which it distributed to sympathetic candidates during that campaign (Sapiro 1986, 136).

The Democratic and Republican parties, well aware of the potential power of the women's vote, responded in kind. The Democratic party nominated Geraldine Ferraro for vice-president in 1984 and adopted a platform designed to appeal to women voters. The Republican party, however, was more threatened. The demands of the women's movement were incompatible with its neo-conservative platform and world view. Neo-conservatives in the United States (as well as Canada and elsewhere) sought to minimize the role of the state in the economy and cut back on social welfare programs. The women's movement, however, demanded increased government intervention and spending on a number of fronts including affirmative action, child care and the feminization of poverty. The Republicans, therefore, attempted to respond to the gender gap by increasing the representation of women within its ranks rather than addressing the substantive concerns of the women's movement. Immediately after the 1980 campaign, Reagan appointed a number of like-minded women to key positions within his administration. At the same time, the Republican party hired pollsters to study women voters and find the subgroups most likely to respond to the Republican message (Mueller 1988, 18, 32). The intent was to deconstruct rather than respond to the gender gap.

Similar patterns emerged in the Canadian electorate as early as the 1979 election, when women appeared slightly more inclined than men to support the federal Liberal party. This gap widened to 6 percent in 1980 and to 10 percent in 1983, after the Liberal government had entrenched a sexual equality clause in the *Canadian Charter of Rights and Freedoms* but when the party had no leader. A gender gap in party choice also materialized in the 1984 federal campaign. Women were 3 percent more likely than men to vote Liberal (Chandler 1990, 29).

Both the American experience and the persistence of a gender gap in the Canadian electorate motivated Canada's federal parties to make special appeals to women in 1984. Each of the major parties doubled their number of women candidates, and a few women were recruited to priority ridings. As important, all of the major parties talked more about women's issues, included specific policies for women in their election platforms and participated in a nationally televised leadership debate devoted exclusively to women's issues.

The experience of the 1984 campaign, however, also demonstrated the instability of the gender gap in the Canadian electorate. Prior to the leadership debate on women's issues, public opinion polls showed that women favoured the Liberal party by a margin of 13 percent. But a week before the election, and after the celebrated leadership debate, this margin all but disappeared. The probable reason is that the leaders of the Liberal and Conservative parties took virtually the same position on all of the issues raised during the night of the debate, ranging from affirmative action to day care to the feminization of poverty. The lack of a clear choice between the two front runners made the women's vote volatile and ultimately susceptible to traditional electoral appeals. In the absence of strong and recognizable differences between the parties on these issues, the voting choices of women are likely to resemble those of men (Carol 1988, 242).

Only the NDP appeared to benefit from women's politicization. This party had targeted women as a potential electoral constituency in the mid-1970s, hiring a full-time organizer to develop the party's responsiveness to women. During the leadership debate on women's issues, the NDP leader also advanced policies most closely resembling the demands of the organized women's movement. This strategy had its rewards for the NDP in 1984 and in 1988. Traditionally, the NDP has received more support from men than women in federal elections. In 1984, however, men and women were equally likely to vote for the party, and between 1984 and 1988 the party increased its support among women by 5 percent (Chandler 1990, 39; Gotell and Brodie 1991).

In a comprehensive analysis of the gender gap in the Canadian federal elections of 1984 and 1988, Celia Chandler found persistent differences in patterns of party support among men and women. In 1988, for example, the differential between female and male support for the Liberal party was 7 percent. However, the largest and most consistent differences are found in relation to a select number of political issues.

In both election years, women were significantly less likely than men to support militarism and significantly more likely to support social welfare spending and women's issues. In 1988 they were also much less likely than men (by a margin of 16 percent) to support the free trade initiative with the United States.

In seeking to explain these differences, Chandler explored three different hypotheses that have been offered as explanations for the gender gap characteristic of many Western democracies. The first hypothesis suggests that women are more likely to defend social welfare measures because they are more often clients of or workers for the welfare state. The second suggests that women and men differ on key issues because of different socialization and life experiences. The third suggests that the second wave of the women's movement, particularly feminist consciousness, leads women and men to evaluate political issues differently. Chandler's study indicates that, while none of the three hypotheses have a high explanatory power, feminist consciousness was particularly important in explaining differences in women's support for social welfare and women's equality issues.

Results from the 1988 National Election Study suggest that slightly less than one-half of Canadian women indicate that they have been

Table 1.7
Selected issue orientations by sex, 1988 Canadian National Election Study
(percent agreeing)

	Women	Men	Feminist women[a]
1. Abortion should be personal choice[b]	48.7	45.6	55.6[c]
2. Government should fund daycare centres	41.3	37.8	48.9[c]
3. Respondent opposes nuclear submarines[b]	67.5	56.1	69.3
4. Government should do more to help			
The poor[b]	82.7	77.5	86.1[c]
Small business	66.7	69.0	66.4
Ethnic minorities[b]	35.5	31.7	44.6[c]
Single parents[b]	66.4	62.3	75.1[c]
Native peoples	50.3	47.6	58.3[c]
The elderly	75.8	74.0	78.4
Women	44.9	39.2	55.1[c]

Source: 1988 Canadian National Election Study.

[a]Feminist women are those scoring above the sample mean on closeness to feminist group scale.
[b]Indicates chi-square statistically significant differences between men and women.
[c]Indicates chi-square statistically significant differences between feminist-leaning and other women.

positively influenced by the women's movement. These feminist women, as shown in tables 1.7 and 1.8, differ significantly both from men and other women in terms of selected issue orientations and political behaviour. Table 1.7 shows that men and women in the electorate differ significantly on issues of reproductive choice, militarism and government support for the poor, ethnic minorities and single parents. Feminist women, however, differ significantly from other women on a broader range of issue positions. They are, for example, much more likely to advocate reproductive choice, government funding for day care and increased government support for almost all the subgroups listed. As in other countries, feminist women appear to occupy a place on the political spectrum that is further to the left than that occupied either by men or women who indicate that they have not been positively influenced by the women's movement.

Table 1.8 shows differences in political participation between women and men, and between feminist and non-feminist women in 1988. The results indicate that men continue to have higher levels of political interest and participation than women. In particular, men are significantly more likely to indicate that they were very interested in the 1988 federal campaign, to have discussed politics during the campaign,

Table 1.8
Orientations toward electoral politics in 1988 by sex
(percentages)

	Women (N = 1 481)	Men (N = 1 441)	Feminist women (N = 616)
1. Interested in election[a]			
Very	35.3	42.1	39.9
Fairly	42.7	40.1	42.9
Not very	17.6	14.2	14.4
Not at all	4.5	3.7	2.8
2. Voted in 1988 election	89.0	87.2	90.4
3. Discussed politics during campaign[a]	74.7	79.5	79.1[b]
4. Helped a party[a]	11.5	14.5	11.9[b]
5. Watched a leadership debate[a]	58.6	67.8	61.4[b]
6. Gave money to candidate or party	24.9	26.9	32.4[b]

Source: 1988 Canadian National Election Study.

[a]Indicates chi-square statistically significant differences between men and women.

[b]Indicates chi-square statistically significant differences between feminist-leaning and other women.

helped a party and watched the leadership debate. However, again, feminist women demonstrate a higher level of politicization than other women along almost every dimension. As important, their participation nearly matches that of men.

In summary, this examination of the behaviour of women in the Canadian electorate indicates that gender differences in citizen participation are no longer sufficient explanations for the virtual exclusion of women from elected office, if indeed they ever were. Canadian women and men are equally likely to vote, and only minor differences in other forms of citizen orientations remain. The fact that a linkage between voting and élite recruitment cannot be established should not be surprising. Voting is a unique form of political behaviour in the sense that it is practised by most but, at the same time, occurs infrequently, and the agenda is largely set by the media and political parties. Nevertheless, the 1980s have witnessed significant changes in the Canadian electorate and elsewhere. After decades of dormancy, gender appears to be increasingly politicized in the Canadian electorate, manifesting itself both in terms of issue orientation and party preference. Although most political parties have been only minimally responsive to the emergence and demands of the women's movement, there is tentative evidence to suggest that many women in the electorate may be ready to mobilize around a party that speaks to their political interests. Existing parties have the option of responding to women as a distinct political constituency or forfeiting these voters to a party that will.

WOMEN IN PARTIES

Although only a fragile and questionable link can be drawn between citizen participation and the political representation of women, the same cannot be said for the relationship between gender biases within political parties and political representation. Within parliamentary systems of government such as Canada's, political parties maintain firm control over the nomination of candidates for elected office. They stand as the gatekeepers to both provincial and federal legislative office and, thus, the representation of women in Canadian legislatures in no small way depends on their experiences within political party organizations. For most of this century, however, Canadian political parties have not been committed to the advancement of women's equality, either within their organizational structures or in the population generally. As Judy LaMarsh observed 20 years ago, "No political party in Canada can claim to be particularly sensitive to the women within its organization, much less to the women in the electorate at large" (quoted in Myers 1989, 49).

The Marginal Partisans

The roots of women's marginalization in partisan politics can be traced back to the very beginnings of the party system. The Canadian party system developed within the context of a very rigid and popular ideology about men's and women's proper roles in society. This ideology revolved around the notion of separate spheres. The public sphere of paid work and politics was assumed to be the appropriate place for men while the private sphere of the home and family was assumed to be most compatible with womanhood. The idea of separate spheres not only barred women from voting and running for office but also informed what were considered to be the legitimate boundaries of political discourse as the Canadian party system took shape. Politics came to be equated with public activity beyond the realm of the domestic sphere. Consequently, Canada's political parties did not even recognize women's concerns as part of the realm of legitimate politics.[3]

The Canadian suffrage movement did little to change a definition of politics constructed within these terms. Although the first wave of Canadian feminism contained many ideological currents, maternal or social feminists dominated the movement. These women (and some men) accepted and propagated the widespread patriarchal assumption of the period that women, by virtue of their reproductive capacity, were more moral, caring and pure than men and thus would help clean up politics and society if granted the vote. Except for the immediate goal of the franchise, women's rights and subordinate social status were of secondary concern. Moreover, many early suffragists saw political parties as bastions of corruption, which "good" women should avoid at all costs.

Women's Auxiliaries

After women's suffrage, Canada's political parties integrated women into the party structure in such a way as to reinforce an ideology of sexual difference and political inequality. Even before their enfranchisement, it was not uncommon to find women performing many of the menial and housekeeping chores of party organization. Their formal recognition in the party structure came with the establishment of women's auxiliaries, appendages to the main party organization. The first women's auxiliary was established in 1913, while the first national organization, the Federation of Liberal Women of Canada, was launched in 1928. Shortly after, the Conservative party established a similar gendered organizational appendage (Gotell and Brodie 1991; Bashevkin 1985, chap. 5; Canada, Royal Commission 1970, 345–50).

Women's auxiliaries were initially conceived as educational forums for newly enfranchised women and quickly expanded to the constituency organizations of both the Conservative and Liberal parties. It was not long, therefore, before a sexual division of labour was firmly entrenched in the organizational structure of both major parties of the period. Women's auxiliaries provided a ready pool of dedicated volunteers during election campaigns and succeeded in impeding women's participation within the mainstream of party organizations (Bashevkin 1985, 100–105). Indeed, the idea that these auxiliaries could act to promote the position of women within party organizations was dismissed by party élites until very recently. As anecdotal evidence of this, in the 1950s Jack Pickersgill, a powerful strategist in the then-governing Liberal party, reflected on the role of women's auxiliaries in the following manner: "I do not think," he said, "a women's organization – I hope it is not – is formed for the purpose of promoting the interests of women." As late as 1968, party officials saw the purpose of women's auxiliaries as providing the labour power for the party at election time. For example, in a Liberal party document entitled "Woman Power," the party instructed campaign managers to use women in committee rooms and in telephone campaigns because "women enjoyed meeting the public and were excellent in this type of work" (Myers 1989, 46, 55).

With the rise of second-wave feminism, women's auxiliaries faced increasing criticism and demands for their abolition. They were indicted for confining women to separate support organizations that were almost entirely dedicated to servicing party committee rooms, canvassing, sponsoring special fund-raising functions and performing many of the necessary but menial tasks of party organization. Women in these organizations, it was argued, were simply volunteers who helped in the election of the party's male candidate. This organizationally entrenched division of labour meant that responsibility for the election strategy, policy development and the disbursement of funds – the élite roles of the party – was assumed by men in the main party structure (Canada, Royal Commission 1970, 346).

Demands for the organizational reform of the two major parties came from many quarters, both inside and outside the parties, and were informed by second-wave feminism. Women's auxiliaries were condemned as discriminatory and antiquated by the Royal Commission on the Status of Women, and many women party activists, usually the young and well educated, lobbied within their parties for their dissolution. All three major parties have responded to these pressures in the past two decades. Separate women's organizations still exist in Canada's major party organizations but their functions within party organizations have changed dramatically in the past decade. Although a few traditional women's clubs remain, especially in rural ridings, most now function as active lobby groups concerned with recruiting more women candidates, sponsoring political-skills seminars and generally promoting the position of women within their party organizations.

Separate women's organizations were never established on a national scale in either the Co-operative Commonwealth Federation (CCF) or its successor, the NDP. Nevertheless, in 1969 the national party established a special committee to respond to the demands of women for increased representation. The Participation of Women Committee (POW) consists of one woman representative from each province and territory. POW generally meets twice a year and focuses its energies on integrating women's concerns into party policy and increasing the number of women NDP candidates for legislative office. The NDP also hired a full-time women's organizer in the mid-1970s.

The Liberal Party of Canada responded to demands for organizational change in 1973. The Women's Liberal Federation of Canada was disbanded and replaced by the Women's Liberal Commission, later (in 1982) renamed the National Women's Liberal Commission. It has 1 national president and 5 regional representatives elected nationally, as well as 12 provincial and territorial presidents who govern more than 150 women's clubs across the country. Their self-expressed mandate is to "represent and promote the interests of women within the Liberal Party and to encourage active participation of women at all levels of party activities" (Liberal Party of Canada, undated).

The national Progressive Conservative party acted in 1981 with the establishment of the Women's Bureau at party headquarters in Ottawa. Special organizations for women within the Conservative party are more varied, containing elements of the old and new. First, there is the National Progressive Conservative Women's Federation (NPCWF), which acts as an umbrella organization within the party and a formal executive structure for the representation of women in the party organization. Its organizational structure resembles its counterpart in the Liberal Party of Canada. Second is the Women's Bureau, which acts as a research and administrative unit for NPCWF. Third, there are 12 city-based women's caucuses, which aim to target and train women for political involvement, especially candidacy. Finally, some 60 riding-based women's associations remain. These groups strongly resemble the women's auxiliaries of before, generally offering riding support rather than political skills training or support for potential women candidates (NPCWF 1989).

For the most part, however, women's party organizations have changed their strategies from getting the party's male candidate elected to advancing the goal of woman's political representation. Nevertheless, as one party spokeswoman recently observed, "Women's organizations have a long way to go before being accorded equal respect and recognition." In fact, in the Conservative party, it has been reported that there is resistance to the idea of expanding the role of women's groups in the party and that many would like to see them disappear.[4]

Women in the Parties

Although party women's groups have shifted their focus to enhancing the status of women in their respective parties, many women party activists now simply by-pass women's organizations and participate directly in the main party structure. Yet, most evidence indicates that their participation, while improving, continues to be circumscribed by an implicit sexual division of labour. There is now an impressive body of research documenting how the structures and practices of Canadian political parties have inhibited women from achieving political power. Regardless of partisan stripe, all of Canada's political parties have consistently reflected "the higher, the fewer," rule: that is, the higher up the party echelon one goes and the more electorally competitive the party, the fewer women are to be found.[5] In recent years, more women have moved into executive positions, especially at the constituency level, but, as Bashevkin discovered, these women usually assume pink-collar positions. Moreover, women are most likely to assume the role of riding president when their party is electorally uncompetitive. A sexual division of labour and power are an integral part of the internal dynamic of most organizations, including political parties.

By most indicators, Canada's political parties have been slow to respond to the demand for women's equality – a position that puts them out of touch with the changing mood of the Canadian electorate. Although there are few data that compare party activists and the general public, one study conducted in the mid-1980s suggests that the gulf between the public and active partisans on women's equality is quite large. This study compares the responses of delegates to the 1983 Progressive Conservative and 1984 Liberal leadership conventions with the 1984 CBC Election Poll. It found that 85 percent of Canadian women and 80 percent of Canadian men agreed with the proposition that "more should be done for women's equality." In stark contrast, only 28 percent of male and 46 percent of female PC delegates, and 38 percent of male and 63 percent of female Liberal delegates, endorsed this view (Brodie 1987).

Women's Representation

The national Liberal and Progressive Conservative parties also have been slow to adopt measures to ensure the representation of women in their organizational hierarchies. The constitutions of both parties declare a commitment to the principle of gender parity within the party organization. Nevertheless, the only explicit guarantees for the representation of women relate either to the representation of the parties' women's groups or to delegate selection for national party conventions. The Liberal party's constitution, for example, guarantees the representation of the National Women's Liberal Commission (NWLC) on the party's national executive, and on 12 of the party's 15 standing committees. In two of the remaining committees, the constitution stipulates that a woman must be represented. The composition of the remaining committee, the National Platform Committee, does not include guarantees either for the representation of the NWLC or individual women. Constitutional provisions for the representation of women within the Conservative party hierarchy are similar. The National Progressive Conservative Women's Federation is ensured representation on the party's three major governing bodies – the national executive, the executive committee and the steering committee.

Both parties guarantee women's representation at national party conventions. The Liberal and Conservative parties adopted constitutional guarantees for representation of women to party conventions in the mid-1960s. At that time both parties introduced a mandatory requirement that at least one convention delegate from each constituency delegation be a woman. Correspondingly, 16.5 percent of the 1967 Progressive Conservative and 15.3 percent of the 1968 Liberal leadership convention delegates were women (Brodie 1987). Since then the rules for delegate selection have been amended. In the Liberal party women are guaranteed representation through party women's groups and in constituency delegations. Each constituency is entitled to 12 delegates, "four of whom shall be men, four of whom shall be women, and four of whom shall be youth (two of whom shall be men and two of whom shall be women)" (Liberal Party of Canada 1986, 16:g). The Conservative party constitution specifies that at least two of the six constituency delegates be women and grants delegate status to the presidents of Conservative women's organizations. These changes, although not formally committed to gender parity, have almost achieved this goal. Women constituted approximately 46 percent of the delegates attending the 1989 federal Progressive Conservative national convention and 47 percent of the 1990 federal Liberal leadership convention (Bashevkin 1991).

Affirmative Action

There is also considerable evidence to suggest that women are moving up the organizational ladder of the Liberal and Conservative parties. In 1990, for example, women held 38 percent of the federal Liberal and 43 percent of the federal Progressive Conservative party executive positions (Bashevkin 1991). Nevertheless, these proportions still fall well below the NDP's 1990 mark of 58 percent. Although the NDP does not guarantee women's representation at national conventions, it stands alone in guaranteeing, in its party constitution, the equal representation of women in the party's hierarchy. In 1983, the NDP became the first party in North America to guarantee gender parity on its executive and all of its governing bodies and committees. In the late 1980s, 7 of the party's 12 vice-presidents were women. Moreover, the party has elected a woman president 4 times in the past 12 years.

While Canadian political parties generally have resisted affirmative action or quota systems, the example of the NDP as well as the international experience suggests that these strategies are becoming increasingly popular mechanisms to correct women's historic disadvantage in partisan politics. As discussed below, many European parties now have in place quota systems to guarantee women's representation on their governing bodies. Nevertheless, even with quotas, there are still substantial obstacles for women, preventing them from rising to the rank of party leader. A woman now leads the federal NDP, and four women have assumed the task of provincial party leader. With the possible exception of the NDP federal leadership, however, all women party leaders in Canada have been elected when their party was electorally uncompetitive. Party leadership positions for competitive federal and provincial parties are highly prized positions and subject to escalating campaign costs. The growing costs of contesting the leadership of a competitive party casts the leadership outside the financial reach of most women aspirants.

Canadian political parties have been silent about the issue of women's representation until very recently. With mounting evidence of a gender gap in the general electorate, parties have begun to open their doors to women. Women now have party constitutional guarantees of representation at national conventions and through representatives of party women's groups. The federal NDP, however, has demonstrated the deepest commitment to women's representation by requiring the equal representation of women on party councils and committees. In turn, this has provided an opportunity structure for women to develop their political skills and contacts, thereby lowering the obstacles to the key partisan posts of party president and party leader (both of which are now held by women).

Political parties do not have to respond to the issue orientations of the women's movement. In fact, as discussed above, neo-conservative parties may be limited in their policy responses because many of the demands of the women's movement are incompatible with the neo-conservatives' goal of reducing the role of government. Nevertheless, the silence of political parties about women increasingly distances them from the mood of the electorate and, thus, becomes one of the factors contributing to the increasing alienation of the Canadian electorate. Moreover, the failure of the Liberal and Conservative parties to control the costs of contesting party leadership both effectively bars most women from achieving this position and fuels public suspicions that politics is only for the rich. Although it is not within the mandate of the Commission to legislate party policy, clearly it is time for the parties to review their orientations toward women in the electorate and within their organizations.

WOMEN AS CANDIDATES

Although women have had the right to compete for federal office for 70 years, their entry into the ranks of Canada's legislative élite has been painfully slow (see table 1.1). In the first 40 years after women's suffrage, women rarely gained their party's nomination for legislative candidacy and even more rarely won election. Indeed, between 1921 and 1968, less than 1 percent of those elected to the House of Commons were women. Although women entered some provincial legislatures more easily in the early years, still, as late as 1983, only 6 percent of a total of 1 172 provincial legislators were women (Brodie 1985, 2). Beginning in the late 1970s, however, Canadian federal politics began to witness a mini-revolution with respect to the political representation of women. Women as a proportion of federal candidates increased from 9 percent in 1974 to 19 percent in 1988. During the same period, their representation in the House of Commons grew from 3 percent to 13 percent. Nevertheless, even though women have significantly increased their participation at this level of electoral politics, the average female candidate has a much lower probability of winning than the average male candidate (see table 1.3). This gender difference can be attributed to two factors. First, until 1984, the majority of female candidates for federal office were affiliated with a minor party and, second, most of the female candidates for one of the three major federal parties ran in lost-cause ridings where their chances for victory were extremely low.

Sacrificial Lambs

Canada's experience during the past two decades very much parallels the international experience. Between 1979 and 1983, for example, the United Kingdom witnessed a virtual doubling in the number of women competing for national office (from 138 to 276) but *no increase* in the number of women elected. This may be because women candidates failed to gain nominations to safe seats (Randall 1987, 139). Similarly, women contesting election for the New Zealand National party have had a lower chance for election than their male counterparts, again because they were unable to win party nominations to competitive ridings (Hill and Roberts 1990, 62). The experience of women in Western liberal democracies has been almost universal. More women are running for legislative office but their gains in representation have been slow and tentative.

In Canada and elsewhere, women often are granted the opportunity to compete for political leadership only when their chances of winning are small. The standard response of party officials to this dilemma traditionally has been that there is a shortage of qualified women to nominate to winnable ridings or that women are an electoral liability and will lose the party votes. Neither argument finds much empirical support. For example, in a study of women candidates competing for provincial and federal office in Canada in the period from 1945 to 1975, statistical analysis shows that a woman's educational or occupational status had nothing to do with whether she secured a party nomination in a competitive or lost-cause riding. Although rarely secured by women, competitive ridings were most often won by women with a history of party service (Brodie 1985, 114).

The widespread assumption that women candidates are an electoral liability also finds little support. Studies from the United States, the United Kingdom and Australia show that there is no electoral risk in running a woman candidate. They conclude that women will be elected when parties select them for winnable seats (Hill and Roberts 1990, 62; Hills 1981). Similar studies are not available for the Canadian case. Nevertheless, leading pollsters agree that a woman's name on a ballot is relevant to the outcome of the election. Indeed, they suggest that it may be an advantage because of the growing importance of family issues in the public mind (*Toronto Star* 1988). American studies also show that voters give women politicians a higher grade than their male counterparts for honesty, intelligence and understanding the voters' needs – all definite advantages in a period of growing voter cynicism (Vancouver *Sun* 1988).

Explaining the Exclusion

Political scientists have tended to explain the exclusion of women from political leadership with two sets of factors. The first set relates to the characteristics of women that impede them from entering the electoral fray, while the second set examines structural and systemic characteristics that discriminate against women. Among the several reasons offered for why women do not contest political office are the contentions that women are inherently less assertive than men; that they are more oriented to the private sphere of the family than the public world of politics; that women do not have the social capital (i.e., relevant skills and networks) to compete in politics; and that early political socialization engenders among girls the idea that politics is an inappropriate feminine activity. Most consistently, however, studies find that situational factors, especially the role of parenthood, more adversely affect the careers of female than male would-be politicians. Women candidates in Canada and elsewhere tend to delay their political careers until their children have grown. The constraints of motherhood in a society that does not provide much recognition for the need for child care may delay a woman's career in politics but does not in and of itself explain why so few women choose a full-time political role later in life (Brodie 1985, 84; Randall 1987, 126). The fact that women tend to delay their entry into politics means that women politicians are disadvantaged in the long climb to political leadership. To get to the top one generally has to start early (Randall 1987, 126).

Proportional Representation

Studies that examine the personal constraints of women's candidacy tend to assume that the electoral system itself does not act to systematically filter women out of representative roles. Political scientists, however, have increasingly pointed to systemic factors as explanations for why women have difficulties gaining election. In particular, statistical analyses show that the type of electoral system is the single most important variable in explaining cross-national variations in women's representation in national assemblies (Norris 1985). Countries that have adopted some form of proportional representation (PR) system consistently elect more women than countries with single-member plurality systems.

There are numerous explanations for why women should fare better in PR systems. In single-member plurality systems, party nominations tend to be the prerogative of local party organizations. It is sometimes argued that discrimination against women is more likely to occur at this level (Lovenduski and Norris 1989, 534). This claim has not been substantiated empirically. Nevertheless, it is the case that PR systems do allow more centralized control of the party nomination lists, thus enabling the national party hierarchy to devise candidate slates that are representative of the main groups in society (Randall 1987, 140–44). Equally important, it is more difficult for parties to exclude women when voters are presented with a list of candidates rather than a ballot that offers a choice among a few competing candidates. The under-representation of women, in other words, is more visible (Vallance and Davies 1986, 36).

On the face of it, women are elected with greater frequency in PR systems (see table 1.4). Support for the efficacy of PR systems also comes from the experience of elections to the European Parliament, which is governed by a proportional system. All European Economic Community (EEC) member countries except Ireland have elected a higher percentage of women to the European Parliament in Strasbourg than are present in their national assemblies (Lovenduski 1986, 208). In some cases, the difference is quite striking. In France, for example, 21 percent of its delegates to the European Parliament are women compared with 4 percent of its national assembly. The former were selected through proportional representation and the latter were elected under a plurality system (Randall 1987, 140). (Australia also elects more women to its Senate, which is governed by the rules of PR, than to its national legislature, which uses a plurality system.) The case of the European Parliament, however, could as easily support the rule that "where power is not, women are" as it can demonstrate the efficacy of PR systems. Put simply, the European Parliament does not have as much power as national assemblies. It does not have legislative power or a ruling party, and decisions are made through compromise and consensus (Vallance and Davies 1986, 33).

Proportional representation systems are not neutral rule systems but, instead, are the products of specific historical cultures. Most commonly, they are found in countries with a long tradition of strong left parties. These parties are more likely than right-wing parties to promote women's issues and women through their ranks (Randall 1987, 108; Gotell and Brodie 1991). Women have fared best in PR systems where the women's movement has put concerted pressure on political parties to elect women. The international experience suggests that women have achieved the greatest measure of political representation when there has been positive intervention to ensure the election of women and the implementation of the goal of gender equality through law (Epstein and Coser 1981, 6). Proportional representation systems may facilitate this goal, but organized pressure from the women's movement is the precondition for reform (Fund for Feminist Majority (FFM) 1988).

The Women's Movement

One of the earliest examples of how the women's movement used a PR system to increase the election of women occurred in Norway in 1967. In an effort to encourage citizen participation in local politics, the election rules were changed to allow voters to cross out names on official candidate slates and replace them with candidates of their own choosing. Women's groups organized a campaign to insert women's names, and in 1971 women won over 50 percent of the seats in three municipalities. This intervention and outcome brought demands to change the rules again to return to the parties their lost power to set the candidate slates. The rules were changed in 1975, and the proportion of women in local government dropped substantially (Katzenstein 1984, 13). Women's groups have also used the PR system, which rewards parties with legislative seats proportional to their popular vote, to launch feminist parties. The greatest success to date has been in Iceland. In 1987, the Women's Alliance party became the first feminist party to win parliamentary seats, six in all, which was sufficient to give the new party the balance of power in the national assembly (Canadian Advisory Council on the Status of Women 1988, 2).

Affirmative Action

The most familiar strategy has been for feminists and their allies to fight within their parties for quotas that ensure women's representation on party lists. For example, in the early 1970s the Swedish Liberal, Social Democratic and Communist parties adopted quota systems to increase women's representation. Later in the decade, the French Socialist Party adopted a quota. Norway's Liberal and Socialist, and the Dutch Labour parties all have established the requirement of a 25 percent female presence at all levels of party life (Randall 1987, 147). The West German Green Party has a 50-50 rule, which includes gender parity both within the party and on party lists, while the West German Social Democratic Party has adopted a 30 percent quota for women's representation within the party. Most significantly, the Norwegian Labour Party adopted a 40 percent rule, now encoded in Norwegian law, which specifies that neither sex should occupy fewer than 40 percent of all the party's posts, including candidates for local and national office (FFM 1988). Norway now leads the Western world in the election of women.

Almost 20 years of experience with some form of affirmative action has led many to conclude that women's representation in political parties and elected assemblies will not be realized without some form of intervention. The Committee on Women's Rights of the European Parliament, for example, concluded that voluntary measures for affirmative action have brought few successes. Therefore, it proposed, and the European Parliament passed, a resolution calling for quota systems and affirmative action programs for women in the internal structures of parties *and* a "monitorable quota system aimed at achieving numerical equality between men and women in all representative political bodies within the foreseeable future" (FFM 1988, 2).

Canada's single-member plurality system and its tradition of local party selection of candidates for legislative office is a formidable obstacle to the implementation of similar quotas. Nevertheless, in 1983–84, each of the major federal parties took tentative steps toward affirmative action by establishing special funds for women candidates. The Progressive Conservatives have established the Ellen Fairclough Foundation, named in honour of the first woman to enter the ranks of the federal cabinet. It is a separate party fund designated to provide training and development programs and provide financial support to women candidates. The Liberal party has established the Judy LaMarsh Fund, which has similar goals. Both funds are given directly to women candidates to help pay for the special financial burdens of women candidates such as child care and housekeeping. The funds are distributed at a base rate and were in the range of $500 in 1984 and $800 in 1988. The NDP's Agnes MacPhail Fund distributes funds to riding associations and not to individual women candidates, and the allocations vary according to need. In 1988, NDP women candidates were given $1 000–$1 500. While these funds provide a token recognition of the special circumstances of women candidates, they rest on an insecure foundation. The moneys collected for these funds come from direct mail and the fund-raising activities of women's party organizations.

Some provincial political parties have followed the lead of their federal counterparts and have established similar special funds for women candidates. In Ontario, for example, the Liberals have established the Margaret Campbell Fund, the NDP has the Women's Electoral Fund (established in 1976) and the Progressive Conservatives had WIN '89. The Conservative fund differs from the others because the assistance is directed to women seeking party nomination rather than provincial election. Considering the growing costs of contesting a party nomination and the fact that electoral financing is partly subsidized with public moneys, special funding at the nomination stage is especially appropriate and is probably the most efficient allocation of these limited resources.

Among Canadian political parties, the Ontario NDP has taken the most significant steps toward affirmative action for women candidates. Although a voluntary program, the party established an affirmative action program in 1989. In addition to setting a spending limit of $5 000 for all candidates seeking nomination, the affirmative action plan specifies that 50 percent of all constituencies should have women candidates, and that 75 percent of priority ridings should be allocated to affirmative action target groups including women. In the 1990 provincial campaign, the party fell short of its goal (30 percent of the Ontario NDP candidates were women), but the nomination of women to priority ridings brought many women (20 out of 74 NDP members) to Queen's Park (Bashevkin 1991).

Pressure from the Outside

Traditionally, in Canada, pressure for reforms for women's advancement has often come from outside rather than inside party organizations. Cross-partisan groups have advocated the advancement of women in Canadian politics since the 1960s. These include the Voice of Women (1960) and the Fédération des femmes du Québec (1966), as well as the Committee for Equality for Women (1966), which successfully pressured the federal government to appoint the Royal Commission on the Status of Women in 1970 (Black 1988, 83). The early 1970s saw the organization of the National Action Committee on the Status of Women (NAC) and the Canadian Advisory Council on the Status of Women (CACSW), both of which have consistently protested the lack of representation of women in Canadian politics. In 1988, the NAC launched a campaign encouraging women to use their vote in support of candidates who opposed the Free Trade Agreement and promised action on reproductive choice, child care and violence against women. Women for Political Action was organized in 1972 to increase women's election through independent candidacies. In the 1980s, however, there has been a proliferation of groups devoted solely to increasing the election of women. These include Canadian Women for Political Representation, the Committee of '94, which has set as its goal the equal representation of women in the House of Commons by 1994, the 52% Solution based in Atlantic Canada, three Quebec-based groups, FRAPPE, FFQ and AFEAS and Winning Women, which has chapters in five provinces (Maillé 1990, 27–28).

The growth of nonpartisan women's groups organized around the goal of increasing the representation and influence of women in Canadian government parallels the American experience. Frustrated with political party and government inaction, women have organized a number of influential groups including the National Organization of Women, the National Women's Political Caucus, the Women's Campaign Fund, and most recently, the Fund for the Feminist Majority. These groups, like those in Canada, have increasingly focused on funding as the major obstacle to women's political advancement and have been successful in raising substantial funds to support women candidates (Sapiro 1986). Ultimately, however, these groups cannot compete with the funds made available to candidates from other sources such as business and political action committees or keep pace with the escalating costs of contesting an election.

Continuing Hurdles

The general consensus among political activists and academics is that, failing the implementation of a quota for women candidates, the most effective way to enable women to compete in electoral politics is to focus on electoral financing. Because women have been segregated in the private sphere and female job ghettos, they neither have the personal financial resources nor the moneyed networks to allow them to compete effectively in increasingly expensive electoral politics. In study after study, women candidates indicate that the most formidable obstacles they encountered in their pursuit for office were winning their party's nomination and financing their campaign.

As discussed earlier, Canadian political parties have tended to nominate women to ridings where their chances of winning were small. Until the 1980s, for example, the majority of women contested federal election for a minor party or as independents. Among those contesting election for one of the three major parties, few gained the nomination where their party had been competitive previously. For example, among a sample of women candidates contesting provincial or federal office in the period between 1945 and 1975, a full 63 percent were nominated to ridings where their party had won none of the past five elections. Moreover, this study found that the more electorally competitive the riding, the more likely the woman candidate was to experience some form of "dirty trick" such as irregularities in voting, opposition from the party hierarchy or finding a male candidate to oppose her (Brodie 1985, 112–13).

Some have assessed the 1984 and 1988 elections as watersheds, marking a significant change in the federal parties' treatment of women candidates. As discussed in the section on Women in the Canadian Electorate, the early 1980s differed from earlier periods because of the apparent emergence of a gender gap in policy and party preference in the Canadian federal electorate. All three major parties entered into a competition for votes by advancing platforms directed at women, by participating in a leadership debate on women's issues and by nominating more women candidates. The 1984 federal election saw, for the first time, more women candidates fielded by the three major parties than by the minor parties. In 1980, the Liberals had 22 women candidates, the Conservatives had 14 and the New Democrats had 33. In 1984, the Liberals had 43, the Conservatives had 23 and the NDP had 65 (Brodie 1985, 125). This trend continued in 1988 when fully 58 percent of the women candidates ran for one of the three major parties. In that election year, the Liberals ran 53 women, the Conservatives ran 37 and the NDP ran 84. Nevertheless, the tendency for women to be nominated disproportionately to less competitive constituencies continued. In 1984, for example, the Conservatives ran most of their women candidates in Quebec where, at the time of their nomination, defeat seemed certain. Many of these women ran again in 1988, thus raising the number of women running in electorally viable seats. Still, only 11 percent of the women nominated by the three parties in 1988 ran in ridings characterized as safe compared with 25 percent of the male candidates (Erickson 1991, table 4.2). A spokeswoman for FRAPPE has assessed the current situation: "The parties cannot afford not to have women candidates, but having candidates does not mean they have to get elected."[6]

Of course, the process of local candidate selection means that central party officials have less control over party nominations than their counterparts in proportional representation systems. Increasingly, however, the control of local nominations also is slipping out of the local party's hands to those who are able to spend to win the nomination contest. Winning the party nomination in a competitive riding has become a major financial obstacle for most would-be political aspirants. Most parties do not have limitations on the amount spent contesting nomination battles, and there are no accurate sources estimating the amount being spent to win a party nomination in a competitive riding. However, it is widely accepted that the cost of competing for nomination in a winnable urban riding may exceed $50 000 (Globe and Mail 1989). This severely disadvantages many groups that have traditionally been under-represented in Canadian politics, particularly women, who, on average, earn 40 percent less than men and who have fewer links to financial backers. Moreover, contributors to nomination contests receive no income tax receipts, and candidates are not reimbursed for a proportion of their expenses. Running for a party nomination in a winnable riding has become a major financial risk that few Canadians, let alone women, are able to afford.

Financial obstacles are an informal but effective way of barring all but a select few from the institutions of representative government. Studies of women candidates show time and again that they see finances

Table 1.9
Biggest obstacle to first victory by member's sex
(percentages)

Factor	Women	Men
Financial	17.2	11.7
Nomination	56.2	41.2
Volunteers	4.8	9.7
Party support	4.8	3.8
Public support	2.4	21.5
Party gender negative	2.4	1.9
Family obligations	9.7	7.8
Work obligations	2.4	3.8

Source: Arend (n.d.).

as the most significant barrier to their electoral success. In the 1945 to 1975 study discussed earlier, finances were selected as the most important factor delaying women's entry into politics, ranking well above job- or family-related concerns (Brodie 1985, 87). In another study of female and male elected members, conducted by Sylvie Arend of Glendon College, women were found to be much more likely than their male counterparts to see winning the nomination and financial factors as the biggest obstacles to their first electoral victory (see table 1.9).

The different rankings attributed to finances and gaining the nomination in both studies may reflect the experiences of different populations. Specifically, the Arend study deals with winners, who, presumably, were more often contesting nomination in competitive ridings. Such nominations are usually hotly contested. Gaining a competitive party nomination cannot be reduced solely to financial considerations, but they are certainly related, especially in an era that has witnessed a rapid and significant escalation in the costs of mounting a campaign for a nomination contest.

In the preparation of this study, 47 of the 300 women contesting the 1988 federal election were interviewed by telephone to assess the importance of money to their campaign. This set a national sample, and candidates for both major and minor parties were interviewed (see appendix). Before exploring the importance of financing, however, a few general observations can be made (see table 1.10). First, for the majority (56 percent), the 1988 federal campaign represented their first bid for elected office. Second, three-quarters were between 31 and 50 years of age. Third, approximately three-quarters of these women were mothers but most of their children had grown. For some 62 percent, the age of their youngest child at the time of the campaign was 15 years or older. Finally, the occupational backgrounds of these candidates indicate that most of these women combined political candidacy with parenting and work-force participation. Moreover, many of these women were employed in fields traditionally associated with the female paid labour force. Some 29 percent came from law and business, fields from which male candidates are often recruited, while 45 percent came from the

Table 1.10
Backgrounds of 1988 federal women candidates
(percentages)

A. Candidate prior to 1988	
Yes	42.5
No	57.5
B. Age	
21–30	4.5
31–40	42.2
41–50	33.3
51–60	13.3
60 +	6.7
C. Mothers	
Yes	72.3
No	27.7
D. Age of youngest child at time of campaign	
Under 1 year	5.8
2–5	8.8
6–10	11.8
11–15	11.8
Over 15 years	61.8
E. Occupation	
Law	2.6
Business	26.1
Education	17.4
Social services	17.4
Technical	10.7
Municipal government	8.6
Farmer	8.6
Homemaker	4.3
Unemployed, retired	4.3

Source: Appendix.

Note: N = 47.

education, social services and technical fields. Only 8 percent indicated that they were not in the paid labour force before their 1988 candidacy.

Biographical data contained in the *Parliamentary Guide* are incomplete, but they do allow us to make some tentative comparisons between female candidates and the women elected in 1988 (see table 1.11). First, the women elected in 1988 were older than the candidate pool. The modal category is 51–60 for the former and 31–40 for the latter. Second, fewer elected women than candidates report having children. Moreover, since only 15 percent of the elected women are younger than 40 years of age, we can assume that few women MPs have young children. Finally, elected women are more likely to be recruited from law and business (46 percent) than from traditional female sectors such as education and social services (23 percent). In other words, elected women are more likely to resemble the profile of elected men than are women candidates.

The primary focus of the telephone interview was to gather information regarding the financial obstacles to women's candidacies in 1988. Table 1.12 lists a number of factors that could provide an obstacle to women candidates. Candidates were asked to assess whether each factor was very important, somewhat important or not important in their experience. The results show that funding was most often selected as very important, distantly followed by lack of public support, lack of media attention and finding volunteers. Unlike the Arend study of elected women, far fewer women candidates indicated that

Table 1.11
Demographic profiles of elected women MPs, 1988
(percentages)

Age*	
Under 40	14.8
41–50	33.4
51–60	40.7
61 and over	11.1
Occupation	
Law	13.5
Business	32.4
Administrator	24.3
Educator	10.8
Social Services	13.5
Other	5.4
MPs reporting children	48.7

Source: *Parliamentary Guide.*

*Missing data excluded.

winning the nomination was very important. This is because only 15 of the 47 women interviewed contested their nomination. Many ran as lost-cause and minor party candidates. Finally, in contrast to much of the literature on women candidates, the majority of the women interviewed indicated that family obligations were not important obstacles in their bid for election.

The candidates were next asked to select which among these factors was the most important obstacle for their candidacy (see table 1.13). Again, funding far outweighed any other factor in the candidate's assessments. Fully 37 percent of the candidates indicated that finding financial resources to contest election was the greatest obstacle in their campaign. This was followed by lack of public support and lack of

Table 1.12
Obstacles to electoral victory: 1988 women federal candidates
(percentages)

Obstacle	Very important	Somewhat important	Not important
Finding funding	57.4 (27)	19.2 (9)	23.4 (11)
Winning nomination	15.8 (3)	26.3 (5)	57.8 (11)
Finding volunteers	27.6 (13)	48.9 (23)	23.4 (11)
Support from party	6.4 (3)	19.2 (9)	74.4 (35)
Party gender negative	6.8 (3)	—	93.2 (41)
Public gender negative	4.2 (2)	25.6 (12)	70.2 (33)
Lack of media	27.6 (13)	23.4 (11)	48.9 (23)
Lack of public support	31.9 (15)	29.8 (14)	38.3 (18)
Family obligations	14.9 (7)	25.5 (12)	59.6 (28)
Work obligations	21.3 (10)	14.8 (7)	63.8 (30)

Source: Appendix.

Note: Numbers in parentheses indicate number of respondents.

Table 1.13
Ranking of most important obstacles among 1988 women candidates
(percentages)

1. Funding	37.0
2. Lack of public support	18.5
3. Support from party	11.1
4. Lack of media coverage	11.1
5. Family obligations	7.4
6. Winning nomination	3.7
7. Finding volunteers	3.7
8. Party gender negative	3.7
9. Work obligations	3.7

Source: Appendix.

media coverage, factors most often selected by minor party candidates. Only 7 percent felt family obligations were most important.

The next series of questions in the interview focused on financial constraints at the nomination stage of their candidacy (see table 1.14). Slightly more than one-half of the candidates indicated that money was an obstacle in gaining the nomination. This finding should be expected since the majority of candidates were acclaimed. Acclaimed or not,

Table 1.14
Controlling nomination expenditures: assessments of 1988 women candidates

	% responding	No. of candidates
A. Money was obstacle in gaining nomination		
Yes	44.6	21
No	55.4	26
B. Money was obstacle among women contesting nomination		
Yes	53.3	8
No	46.7	7
C. Government should limit amount spent for nomination contest		
Yes	93.6	44
No	6.4	3
D. Suggested expenditure limit for nomination		
Below $5 000	78.6	
$6 000–10 000	21.4	
Above $10 000	—	

Source: Appendix.

94 percent of the candidates agreed that the government should set limits on the amount of money spent during a nomination contest. Moreover, almost 80 percent suggested that this limit should be set below $5 000. None of the candidates suggested that the limit be over $10 000.

Three-quarters of the women candidates indicated that women have special financial burdens when seeking election (see table 1.15). The candidates identified several reasons for why financing was a special problem for women. First, many identified the costs of child care, the carrying costs of homemaking, and the expense of buying clothes for the campaign. Second, they pointed out that more women than men have low-paying jobs, less financial security, and greater difficulties securing a bank loan. Third, many suggested that men have greater access to business contacts, corporate donors and moneyed networks.

Nevertheless, while most of the women candidates saw that women were disadvantaged in financing a campaign, 57 percent disagreed that the government should establish special incentives for women candidates through electoral financing legislation. The reasons most often cited for rejecting this alternative were that affirmative action for women was the legitimate domain of political parties, not government, and that women would be stigmatized by special incentives. In contrast, the 43 percent who did approve of special incentives indicated they were necessary, at least in the short term, to realize the goal of gender equality in Canadian politics.

Almost all (93 percent) of the major national party candidates received funding from one of the party's special funds. NDP candidates

Table 1.15
Incentives for women candidates

A. Women have special financial obstacles when seeking election		
Yes		74.5
No		25.5
B. Government should establish incentives for women candidates through electoral financing legislation		
Yes		42.6
No		57.4
C. Recipient of special funds from parties	Major party	Minor Party
Yes	93.3	—
No	6.7	100.0

Source: Appendix.

Note: Figures represent percentage of candidates responding to questionnaire.

indicated that they received amounts ranging from $1 000–$1 500 while Liberal and Conservative candidates got sums in the range of $700–$850. Most of the candidates indicated that these funds were welcome but not sufficient to have an impact on the campaign. The candidates indicated that the funds were used to partially cover the cost of a nanny, other forms of child care, day-to-day incidentals and wardrobe requirements. None suggested that the parties should not have this special fund for women candidates.

In summary, women continue to face numerous obstacles in their quest for election. Although Canadian political parties now boast more women candidates and elected members than ever before, women continue to be nominated in ridings where their chances for election are small. Women's representational gains have been small and unpredictable. There is no reason to assume that they will continue in the future. The international experience shows that affirmative action programs have been effective mechanisms for realizing the election of women. Short of such a commitment, however, the system remains biased against women and other groups who are unable to compete in increasingly costly electoral politics. In particular, the rising cost of contesting a party nomination rules out the potential candidacies of many women.

CONCLUSION

Historically, women have been under-represented in liberal democratic politics on both a vertical and horizontal plane. On the vertical axis, fewer and fewer women are represented in the agenda-setting and decision-making structures as one moves up the hierarchy of political office and political power. On the horizontal axis, one finds a virtual silence and political inertia on issues that affect the daily lives of many women, especially those emanating from the domestic sphere (Dahlerup 1982, 164). In other words, women are under-represented both in *form* (i.e., to be among those in control of public affairs) and in *content or result* (i.e., the substantive values that politics puts into effect) (Jonasdottir 1988, 40).

It is often assumed that there is little relationship between the form and content of women's political representation. Although it is widely recognized that women rarely assume the role of political decision maker in Canadian society, this fundamental gender gap in the distribution of political power is generally thought to have little impact on the output of the legislative process. It is often argued, for example, that elected representatives, regardless of their gender, function to represent the interests of all of their constituents, including women. In addition, it is suggested that women, as a collectivity, do not have special or objective interests independent of men, the economy or the family and, therefore, do not require corporate representation. Finally, it is suggested that it is impossible to represent women's interests because women themselves do not speak as a collective voice in matters of public policy.

But these explanations for why we should not be concerned with the issue of women's political representation are problematical. First, the legitimacy and efficacy of our representational institutions and the democratic election process are not solely a matter of whether Canada's multiple political interests are aired in a public forum. It is of equal importance that our institutions reflect the composition of the Canadian population and that our rule systems do not prohibit large segments of society from participating in the democratic decision-making process. Second, the argument that women do not need special representation because they do not share the same objective interests or subjective orientations toward politics is gender-biased in its conception. A strong case can be made for seeing women as a special social interest, and there is growing evidence in public opinion data that many women share a collective identity. The fundamental point, however, is that neither of these tests are applied to men. Women, like men, should be able to access the political system to achieve policy goals and to resolve political conflicts regardless of whether these conflicts arise between men and women or, indeed, among women themselves. The argument that women must somehow form a homogeneous bloc of political actors before they are recognized in the political process is a sexist assumption and denies the diversity of women's experience. It is also a fallacy to assume that if gender is not politicized then it is irrelevant to the understanding of politics. The most significant gender gap in Canadian society remains the glaring imbalance between men and women in the distribution and exercise of political power (Mueller 1988, 10).

The question of how to increase women's political representation is complex and long overdue. The history of liberal democracies, however, suggests that granting women formal equality with men and enacting so-called neutral electoral procedures is not sufficient to achieve this goal. At best, the representational advances made by women in the last decade are only tentative. At the present rate of increase, it still would take another nine elections, or nearly 45 years, before men and women were equally represented in the House of Commons (Maillé 1990, 10).

History tells us that formal equality guaranteeing procedural fairness in the electoral system does not produce gender parity in our representative institutions in the context of persistent social and political inequalities. International experience shows us that the greatest gains in women's representation have occurred when political parties and governments have intervened to put women into the position they should have been in at the mythical beginnings of liberal democracy (Clark 1988, 271). Affirmative action policies designed to increase the political representation of women are consistent with both the prescriptions of the *Canadian Charter of Rights and Freedoms* and the evolution of Canadian electoral regulation, which has sought to preserve and expand the integrity of the democratic process. The appointment of the Royal Commission on Electoral Reform and Party Financing provides an opportunity to begin to address the historical legacy of gender bias in the Canadian democratic system.

RECOMMENDATIONS

"Everyone agrees that equality is a good thing – that we must have equality provided that it doesn't cost anything, as long as it will require only superficial changes, provided that we need to do nothing more than make pretty speeches, or as long as it is women who pay the price for it" (the former chairwoman of the Swedish Equality Commission) (Dahlerup 1982, 34).

It is not within the power or mandate of the Royal Commission on Electoral Reform and Party Financing to reverse centuries of gender-based discrimination. It can, however, adopt reforms that recognize and help erode the systemic barriers that have served to exclude women from the process of democratic representation. The Commission has heard briefs from numerous individuals and organizations recommending potential avenues for reform. These include fundamental systemic changes such as the adoption of a proportional representation system of election for the House of Commons (and the Senate), the prohibition of corporate donations to political parties and the establishment of dual-member constituencies, each of which would elect one man and one woman to the House of Commons. The majority of the submissions, however, focused on how financing regulations could be reformed to place women and men more or less on a level playing field in the electoral process. The results of this study also show that financing remains a significant obstacle for women competing in a single-member plurality system. Following from these sources, therefore, this submission to the Royal Commission recommends that:

1. Spending limits should be set at approximately $200 000 for party leadership contests.
2. Spending limits should be set at approximately $5 000 for constituency nomination contests.

3. Contributions for nomination contests should be tax deductible.
4. Campaign expenses for nomination contests should be fully disclosed.
5. Spending for nomination contests should be eligible for reimbursement if the candidate achieves a minimum level of support such as 15 percent of the nomination meeting.
6. Child care and housekeeping should be included as legitimate campaign expenses for both nomination contests and general elections.
7. Legislation should be introduced allowing candidates the right to take unpaid leave from their employment to contest either party nominations or general elections.
8. The Commission should use its mandate in an affirmative manner to realize the goal of electing women by adjusting upward, on a sliding scale, the campaign expenses reimbursed to political parties according to the proportion of their *elected* candidates who are women. This innovation, which could be used to promote the political representation of other disadvantaged groups, would motivate political parties to nominate more women to competitive ridings.

APPENDIX

During July 1990, 47 of the 300 women contesting the 1988 federal election were interviewed by telephone to explore the issue of financing. The following is the questionnaire employed.

Questionnaire

1. First of all, for what party did you run during the 1988 general election?

   _____

   1a. Were you a candidate for election before 1988?_____

   (If yes) For federal, provincial or municipal election?_____

   Were you successful at that time?_____

2. What age were you during the 1988 general election campaign?

   _____

3. What was your occupation at the time of the 1988 general election?

   _____

4. Did you have any children at home at the time of the campaign?

   _____

5. What was the age of your youngest child at the time of the 1988 election campaign?

_____

6. Did you contest the nomination for your party, or were you acclaimed as your party's candidate?

_____

7. Now I'd like to mention some factors which are sometimes seen as obstacles to achieving an electoral victory. For each, could you tell me if it was a major obstacle, somewhat of an obstacle, or not at all an obstacle?

	Major	Somewhat	Not at all
a. finding sources of funding	❏	❏	❏
b. winning local nomination	❏	❏	❏
c. finding volunteers	❏	❏	❏
d. getting support from party	❏	❏	❏
e. party negative to gender	❏	❏	❏
f. public negative to gender	❏	❏	❏
g. lack of media coverage	❏	❏	❏
h. lack of public support	❏	❏	❏
i. family obligations	❏	❏	❏
j. work obligations	❏	❏	❏

8. Of these, which was the biggest obstacle for you?

_____

9. Going back to your 1988 candidacy, which of the following encouraged you to run?

	Yes	No
a. own initiative	❏	❏
b. local party association	❏	❏
c. higher level party member	❏	❏
d. family	❏	❏
e. friends	❏	❏
f. work associates	❏	❏
g. women's organizations	❏	❏
h. other – please specify	❏	❏

10. What was the biggest obstacle to getting the nomination in your riding?

_____

11. Where would you rank money as an obstacle to getting the nomination?

_____

12. Should the government limit the amount of money a candidate can spend at the nomination stage?

  ❐ Yes   ❐ No

13. What would you see as a reasonable limit?

  ❐ less than $5 000

  ❐ $6 000–$10 000

  ❐ $11 000–$15 000

  ❐ more than $15 000

14. Do you think that women candidates have special financial obstacles when seeking election?

_____

  Could you cite a few which you think are important?

_____

  Which is the most important?

_____

15. (If a member of tiny party) Do you think that it is easier for a woman to gain the party nomination for parties such as yours (name) than one of the three major parties?

_____

16. Do you think that the government should establish incentives through its electoral financing legislation to encourage the parties to nominate more women candidates?

  ❐ Yes   ❐ No

17. What kind of incentives?

_____

18. Were you a recipient of special funding from your party because you were a woman candidate?

  ❐ Yes   ❐ No

  18a. What kind of funding?

    the special funds, e.g., Agnes MacPhail_____

    other – specify_____

18b. How important was this funding to your candidacy?

_____

19. Do you have any suggestions about how to increase the election of women?

_____

20. Do you think that electing more women matters?

☐ Yes ☐ No

Why?_____

21. How strongly would you say that you have been influenced by feminism?

☐ Very ☐ Somewhat ☐ Not very

Thank you very much for your time.

NOTES

1. In many of these early electoral regimes women with property – a select group – were allowed to vote, but were few in number, and, in most cases, this privilege was eventually revoked.

2. The term gladiator itself reflects an implicit assumption that the top level is occupied by men.

3. For broader discussion see Gotell and Brodie (1991).

4. These observations were made by Judith Hendin, the outgoing president of the NPCWF. See the *Globe and Mail*, 11 May 1989.

5. Ibid., p. 69; see also Brodie (1987).

6. D. Debbas, FRAPPE, quoted in the *Globe and Mail*, 10 November 1988.

BIBLIOGRAPHY

Adamson, Nancy, Linda Briskin and Margaret McPhail. 1988. *Feminist Organizing for Change.* Toronto: Oxford University Press.

Andrew, Caroline. 1984. "Women and the Welfare State." *Canadian Journal of Political Science* 17:667–83.

Arend, Sylvie. n.d. "The Roads to Electoral Victory." Toronto: York University, Glendon College.

Bacchi, Carol. 1983. *Liberation Deferred? The Ideas of English Canadian Suffragists 1877–1918.* Toronto: University of Toronto Press.

Bashevkin, Sylvia. 1985. *Toeing the Lines: Women and Party Politics in English Canada.* Toronto: University of Toronto Press.

————. 1989. "Political Parties and the Representation of Women." In *Canadian Parties in Transition: Discourse, Organization and Representation,* ed. Alain G. Gagnon and Brian Tanguay. Scarborough: Nelson Canada.

————. 1991. "Women's Participation in Political Parties." In *Women in Canadian Politics: Toward Equity in Representation,* ed. Kathy Megyery. Vol. 6 of the research studies of the Royal Commission on Electoral Reform and Party Financing. Ottawa and Toronto: RCERPF/Dundurn.

Black, Jerome, and Nancy McGlen. 1979. "Male-Female Political Involvement Differentials in Canada, 1965–1974." *Canadian Journal of Political Science* 12:471–97.

Black, Naomi. 1988. "The Canadian Women's Movement: The Second Wave." In *Changing Patterns: Women in Canada,* ed. S. Burt, L. Code and L. Dorney. Toronto: McClelland and Stewart.

Brodie, Janine. 1985. *Women and Politics in Canada.* Toronto: McGraw-Hill Ryerson.

————. 1987. "The Gender Factor in National Party Conventions." In *Party Democracy in Canada,* ed. George Perlin. Toronto: Prentice-Hall.

Brodie, Janine, and Jane Jenson. 1989. *Crisis, Challenge and Change: Party and Class in Canada Revisited.* Ottawa: Carleton University Press.

Brodie, Janine, and Jill Vickers. 1982. *Canadian Women in Politics: An Overview.* Ottawa: Canadian Research Institute for the Advancement of Women.

Burt, Sandra. 1986. "Women's Issues and the Women's Movement in Canada since 1970." In *The Politics of Gender, Ethnicity and Language in Canada.* Vol. 34 of the research studies of the Royal Commission on the Economic Union and Development Prospects for Canada. Toronto: University of Toronto Press.

————. 1990a. "Canadian Women's Groups in the 1980s: Organizational Development and Policy Influence." *Canadian Public Policy* 16:17–28.

————. 1990b. "Rethinking Canadian Politics: The Impact of Gender." In *Canadian Politics in the 1990s.* 3d ed., ed. M. Whittington and G. Williams. Scarborough: Nelson Canada.

————. 1990c. "The Second Wave of the Canadian Women's Movement." In *Canadian Politics: An Introduction to the Discipline,* ed. A.G. Gagnon and J. Bickerton. Peterborough: Broadview Press.

Burt, Sandra, Lorraine Code and L. Dorney. 1988. *Changing Patterns: Women in Canada.* Toronto: McClelland and Stewart.

Canada. Royal Commission on the Status of Women. 1970. *Report.* Ottawa: Information Canada.

Canadian Advisory Council on the Status of Women. 1987. *Women in Politics: Becoming Full Partners in the Political Process*. Background paper. Ottawa: CACSW.

————. 1988. *The Reality Gap*. Ottawa: CACSW.

Canadian Research Institute for the Advancement of Women. 1986. *Women's Involvement in Political Life: A Pilot Study*. Ottawa: CRIAW.

Carol, Susan. 1988. "Women's Autonomy and the Gender Gap: 1980 and 1982." In *The Politics of the Gender Gap: The Social Construction of Political Influence*, ed. Carol Mueller. Newbury Park, CA: Sage Publications.

Chandler, Celia. 1990. "Gender Gap: 1984 and 1988 Canadian General Elections." M.A. research paper, York University.

Clark, L. 1988. "Liberty, Equality, Fraternity – and Sorority." In *Legal Theory Meets Legal Practice*, ed. Anne Bayefsky. Edmonton: Academic Printing and Publishing.

Cleverdon, Catherine. 1974. *Woman Suffrage Movement in Canada*. Toronto: University of Toronto Press.

Costain, Anne. 1988. "Representing Women: The Transition from Social Movement to Interest Groups." In *Women, Power and Policy: Toward the Year 2000*, ed. Ellen Boneparth and Emily Stoper. New York: Pergamon Press.

Dahlerup, Drude. 1982. "Overcoming the Barriers: An Approach to the Study of How Women's Issues Are Kept from the Political Agenda." In *Women's Views of the Political World of Men*, ed. J. Stiehm. New York: Transitional Publishers.

Devere, H. 1990. "Women and the First Labor Government of New Zealand." Paper presented to the Canadian Political Science Association Annual Meeting, Victoria.

Dumont, M. 1986. "The Women's Movement: Then and Now." *Feminist Perspectives*. No. 56. Ottawa: Canadian Research Institute for the Advancement of Women.

Duverger, M. 1955. *The Political Role of Women*. Paris: Unesco.

Eichler, Margrit. 1979. *Sex Equality and Political Participation of Women in Canada: Some Survey Results*. POW Canada Report (1). Toronto: Ontario Institute for Studies in Education.

Eisenstein, Z. 1981. *The Radical Future of Liberal Feminism*. New York: Longman.

————. 1982. "The Sexual Politics of the New Right: Understanding the Crisis of Liberalism." *Feminist Theory* 7:567–88.

Epstein, Cynthia Fuch, and Rose Laub Coser. 1981. *Access to Power: Cross National Studies of Women and Elites.* Boston: Allen and Unwin.

Erickson, Lynda. 1991. "Women and Candidacies for the House of Commons." In *Women in Canadian Politics: Toward Equity in Representation,* ed. Kathy Megyery. Vol. 6 of the research studies of the Royal Commission on Electoral Reform and Party Financing. Ottawa and Toronto: RCERPF/Dundurn.

Evans, Judith. 1980. "Women and Politics: A Re-appraisal." *Political Studies* 28 (2): 210–21.

Fletcher, F.J., and R.J. Drummond. 1979. "Canadian Attitude Trends 1960–1978." Working Paper 4. Montreal: Institute for Research on Public Policy.

Fund for the Feminist Majority. 1988. "The Feminization of Power: An International Comparison." Washington, DC: FFM.

Gelb, Joyce. 1986. "Feminism in Britain: The Politics of Isolation." In *Research in Politics and Society,* vol. 2, ed. Given Moore and Glenna Spitze. London: JAI Press.

Ginsberg, B. 1982. *The Consequences of Consent: Elections, Citizen Control and Popular Acquiescence.* Reading, MA: Addison-Wesley.

Globe and Mail, 10 August 1989.

Globe and Mail, 25 August 1989, A12.

Goldfarb, Martin, and Thomas Axworthy. 1988. *Marching to a Different Drummer.* Toronto: Stoddart.

Gotell, Lise, and Janine Brodie. 1991. "Women and Politics: More Than an Issue of Numbers." In *Party Politics in Canada.* 6th ed., ed. Hugh Thorburn. Toronto: Prentice-Hall.

Haavio-Mannila, Elina, et al., eds. 1985. *Unfinished Democracy: Women in Nordic Politics.* Toronto: Pergamon Press.

Hill, Roberta, and Nigel Roberts. 1990. "Success, Swing and Gender: The Performance of Women Candidates for Parliament in New Zealand, 1946–87." *Politics* 25 (May): 62–80.

Hills, Jill. 1981. "Candidates: The Impact of Gender." *Parliamentary Affairs* 34:221–28.

Iglitzin, Lynne, and Ruth Ross, eds. 1976. *Women of the World.* Santa Barbara: Clio Books.

Jonasdottir, Anna. 1988. "On the Concept of Interest, Women's Interests and the Limitations of Interest Theory." In *The Political Interests of Gender,* ed. Kathleen Jones and Anna Jonasdottir. Newbury Park, CA: Sage Publications.

Jones, Kathleen. 1988. "Toward the Revision of Politics." In *The Political Interests of Gender*, ed. Kathleen Jones and Anna Jonasdottir. Newbury Park, CA: Sage Publications.

Jones, Kathleen, and Anna Jonasdottir, eds. 1988. *The Political Interests of Gender*. Newbury Park, CA: Sage Publications.

Katzenstein, M. 1984. "Feminism and the Meaning of the Vote." *Signs* 10 (1): 4–26.

Kay, Barry, Ronald Lambert, Steven Brown and James Curtis. 1987. "Gender and Political Activity in Canada, 1965–1984." *Canadian Journal of Political Science* 20:851–63.

———. 1988. "Feminist Consciousness and the Canadian Electorate: A Review of the National Election Studies, 1965–1984." *Women and Politics* 8 (2): 1–21.

Kealey, Linda, ed. 1979. *A Not Unreasonable Claim: Women and Reform in Canada, 1880s–1920s*. Toronto: Women's Press.

Kirkpatrick, Jeane. 1976. *The New Presidential Elite*. New York: Russell Sage Foundation.

Kome, Penney. 1989. *Every Voice Counts: A Guide to Personal and Political Action*. Ottawa: Canadian Advisory Council on the Status of Women.

Liberal Party of Canada. Undated. "The Story of the National Liberal Commission." Ottawa.

———. 1986. *Constitution*. Ottawa.

Lovenduski, Joni. 1986. *Women and European Politics*. London: Wheatsheaf Books.

Lovenduski, Joni, and Pippa Norris. 1989. "Selecting Women Candidates: Obstacles to the Feminisation of the House of Commons." *European Journal of Political Research* 17:533–62.

Mackerras, Malcolm. 1980. "Do Women Candidates Lose Votes? Further Evidence." *The Australian Quarterly* 52:450–55.

Macpherson, C.B. 1977. *The Life and Times of Liberal Democracy*. Toronto: Oxford University Press.

Maillé, Chantal. 1990. "Primed for Power: Women in Canadian Politics." Background paper prepared for the Canadian Advisory Council on the Status of Women. Ottawa.

McCormack, Thelma. 1989. "Examining the Election Entrails: Whatever Happened to the Gender Gap." *This Magazine* (March–April): 31–35.

Means, Ingunn. 1976. "Scandinavian Women." In *Women in the World*, ed. Lynn Iglitzin and Ruth Ross. Santa Barbara: Clio Books.

Mendelson, Johanna. 1988. "The Ballot Box Revolution: The Drive to Register Women." In *The Politics of the Gender Gap: The Social Construction of Political Influence,* ed. Carol Mueller. Newbury Park, CA: Sage Publications.

Milbrath, Lester. 1965. *Political Participation.* Chicago: Rand McNally.

Mishler, William. 1979. *Political Participation in Canada.* Toronto: Macmillan.

Molyneux, Maxine. 1986. "Mobilization without Emancipation? Women's Interests, State and Revolution." In *Transition and Development: Problems of Third World Socialism,* ed. R. Fagen et al. New York: Monthly Review.

Mueller, Carol, ed. 1988. *The Politics of the Gender Gap: The Social Construction of Political Influence.* Newbury Park, CA: Sage Publications.

Myers, P. 1989. "A Noble Effort: The National Federation of Liberal Women of Canada, 1928–1973." In *Beyond the Vote: Canadian Women and Politics,* ed. L. Kealey and J. Sangster. Toronto: University of Toronto Press.

National Progressive Conservative Women's Federation. 1989. "Initiatives: A Strategic Plan Towards 1990." Ottawa.

Norris, P. 1985. "Women's Legislative Participation in Western Europe." *West European Politics* 4:90–101.

Pateman, Carole. 1980. "Women, Nature and Suffrage." *Ethics* 90 (July): 564–75.

––––––. 1985. *The Sexual Contract.* Cambridge: Polity Press.

Peattie, Lisa, and Martin Rein. 1983. *Women's Claims: A Study in Political Economy.* London: Oxford University Press.

Pitkin, Hanna. 1967. *The Concept of Representation.* Los Angeles: University of California Press.

––––––. 1968. "Commentary: The Paradox of Representation." In *Representation,* ed. Roland Pennock. New York: Atherton Press.

Prentice, A., et al. 1988. *Canadian Women: A History.* Toronto: Harcourt Brace Jovanovich.

Putnam, Robert. 1976. *The Comparative Study of Political Elites.* Englewood Cliffs: Prentice-Hall.

Randall, Vicky. 1987. *Women and Politics: An International Perspective.* 2d ed. London: Macmillan.

Rogers, Barbara. 1983. *Getting Women's Power into Politics.* London: Women's Press.

Sapiro, Virginia. 1986. "The Women's Movement, Politics and Policy in the Reagan Era." In *The New Women's Movement,* ed. D. Dahlerup. Beverly Hills: Sage Publications.

Schwartz, Nancy. 1988. *The Blue Guitar: Political Representation and Community.* Chicago: University of Chicago Press.

Scott, Joan. 1986. "Gender as a Useful Category in Historical Analysis." *American Historical Review* 91:1055–75.

Siim, Birte. 1988. "Toward a Feminist Rethinking of the Welfare State." In *The Political Interests of Gender,* ed. Kathleen Jones and Anna Jonasdottir. Newbury Park, CA: Sage Publications.

Smart, Carol. 1989. *Feminism and the Power of the Law.* London: Routledge.

Stiehm, Judith. 1981. "Women and Citizenship: Mobilization, Participation, Representation." In *Women, Power and Political Systems,* ed. M. Rendel. London: Croom Helm.

Terry, John. 1984. "The Gender Gap: Women's Political Power." Ottawa: Library of Parliament Research Branch.

Therborn, G. 1977. "The Rule of Capital and the Rise of Democracy." *New Left Review* (June): 3–41.

Toronto Star, 28 May 1988.

Vallance, Elizabeth, and Elizabeth Davies. 1986. *Women of Europe: Women MEPs and Equality Policy.* Cambridge: Cambridge University Press.

Vancouver *Sun,* 9 July 1988.

Vickers, Jill M. 1989. "Feminist Approaches to Women in Politics." In *Beyond the Vote: Canadian Women and Politics,* ed. L. Kealey and J. Sangster. Toronto: University of Toronto Press.

Walzer, Michael. 1984. "Liberalism and the Art of Separation." *Political Theory* (August): 315–30.

Welch, Susan, and Timothy Bledsoe. 1986. "Differences in Campaign Support for Male and Female Candidates." In *Research in Politics and Society,* vol. 2, ed. Given Moore and Glenna Spitze. London: JAI Press.

2

WOMEN'S PARTICIPATION IN POLITICAL PARTIES

Sylvia Bashevkin

P REVIOUS RESEARCH ON women's party involvement has focused on two main themes: first, the higher the fewer; and second, the more competitive the fewer (Bashevkin 1985, chap. 3). This paper examines female participation during the late 1980s through 1990 using that same thematic basis. It compares contemporary data on political engagement with older figures from the late 1970s and early 1980s, questioning the following: Do large numbers of party women remain confined to "pink-collar" work, where they are more likely than party men to fulfil clerical rather than decision-making functions in local riding organizations? What changes have occurred at intermediate levels of party participation, notably in convention delegate, party executive and campaign management roles? Are more women active at the élite level, contesting public office, holding legislative office and obtaining cabinet and party leadership positions than in the past? What factors help to account for improvements in women's numerical representation in party organizations, and what obstacles remain? In examining the last question, this study considers the role of party women's organizations in affecting participation and introduces comparative data to place Canadian findings in a cross-cultural context.

This discussion thus situates questions about female participation in a broad institutional context. It views parties as hierarchically organized pyramids, with a wide base of occasional volunteer activists and an increasingly narrow band of part-time intermediate and then full-time élite participants. As the empirical data that follow demonstrate, women's numerical representation in these organizations tends to be inversely related to both the level of party activity and to the competitive position of a party organization.

LOCAL PARTY ACTIVITY

Canadian women have long done what Judy LaMarsh, the late Liberal MP and cabinet minister, described as the "real donkey-work" for local party organizations, including looking after party minutes, memberships and much of the routine campaign work that was conducted at election time at the constituency level (1969, 282). Anecdotal evidence from activists in all three major federal organizations suggests that as greater numbers of Canadian women have entered the paid labour force, much of this reliable volunteer base has eroded. For example, many local party campaigns have shifted from being primarily daytime committee-room organizations staffed by women and directed by men, to becoming evening committee-room organizations where women expect to find opportunities to staff as well as direct the operations.

Yet, have women escaped the traditional clerical and routine party roles that were referred to in earlier work as the "pink-collar ghetto" (Bashevkin 1985, 57–60)? According to federal data presented in table 2.1 and more complete Ontario provincial figures in table 2.2, large numbers of Canadian women continue to fulfil primarily secretarial functions in local party executives.[1] Approximately two-thirds of constituency secretaries in most parties in which a thorough count has been conducted were female, and this appears to be the case regardless of level of government (federal versus provincial), geographical location or time period. For example, Ontario provincial data from 1988 and 1990 indicate that between one-half and three-quarters of local secretaries were female, and this is similar to patterns present 10 years earlier. As one party activist reflected in 1990, "There are still lots and lots of women in riding secretary positions."

Does this pink-collar phenomenon mean that relatively few women obtain higher levels of local party office? Cell entries in tables 2.1 and 2.2 indicate that, in both the federal and Ontario provincial systems, the numbers and percentages of women who held local president and treasurer/chief financial officer (CFO) positions were far lower than the numbers and percentages for constituency secretary. Table 2.2, for example, shows that between 22 and 35 percent of local Ontario provincial presidents in 1990 were female, as compared with between 14 and 29 percent in 1981. In the case of treasurer/CFO positions, levels in 1990 were between 17 and 29 percent as compared with a range of 12 to 42 percent in 1981.

Table 2.1
Local party participation of women in Canada, federal level, 1990

Province/Territory and number of ridings	Riding position	Liberal		NDP		Progressive Conservative	
		%	N	%	N	%	N
British Columbia 32	President	18.8	(6)	34.4	(11)	9.4	(3)
	Treasurer/CFO	34.4	(11)	56.3	(18)	28.1	(9)
	Secretary	68.8	(22)	68.8	(22)	50.0	(16)
Yukon & NWT 3	President	0.0	(0)	33.3	(1)	0.0	(0)
	Treasurer/CFO	0.0	(0)	33.3	(1)	66.7	(2)
	Secretary	66.7	(2)	33.3	(1)	66.7	(2)
Alberta 26	President	26.9	(7)	23.1	(6)	11.5	(3)
	Treasurer/CFO	23.1	(6)	38.5	(10)	15.4	(4)
	Secretary	50.0	(13)	26.9	(7)	61.5	(16)
Saskatchewan 14	President	14.3	(2)	14.3	(2)	14.3	(2)
	Treasurer/CFO	0.0	(0)	42.9	(6)	7.1	(1)
	Secretary	100.0	(14)	50.0	(7)	85.7	(12)
Manitoba 14	President	28.6	(4)	14.3	(2)	7.1	(1)
	Treasurer/CFO	28.6	(4)	28.6	(4)	21.4	(3)
	Secretary	42.9	(6)	64.3	(9)	64.3	(9)
Ontario 99	President	28.3	(28)	30.3	(30)	22.2	(22)
	Treasurer/CFO	n.a.		29.3	(29)	14.1	(14)
	Secretary	n.a.		46.5	(46)	65.7	(65)
Quebec 75	President	22.7	(17)	14.7	(11)	8.0	(6)
	Treasurer/CFO	n.a.		n.a.		30.7	(23)
	Secretary	n.a.		n.a.		64.0	(48)
New Brunswick 10	President	20.0	(2)	40.0	(4)	30.0	(3)
	Treasurer/CFO	30.0	(3)	40.0	(4)	20.0	(2)
	Secretary	80.0	(8)	50.0	(5)	90.0	(9)
Nova Scotia 11	President	27.3	(3)	27.3	(3)	9.1	(1)
	Treasurer/CFO	n.a.		45.5	(5)	9.1	(1)
	Secretary	n.a.		36.4	(4)	54.6	(6)
Prince Edward Island 4	President	0.0	(0)	0.0	(0)	0.0	(0)
	Treasurer/CFO	50.0	(2)	25.0	(1)	25.0	(1)
	Secretary	75.0	(3)	75.0	(3)	100.0	(4)

Table 2.1 (cont'd)

Province/Territory and number of ridings	Riding position	Liberal		NDP		Progressive Conservative	
		%	N	%	N	%	N
Newfoundland 7	President	14.3	(1)	14.3	(1)	n.a.	
	Treasurer/CFO	n.a.		0.0	(0)	57.1	(4)
	Secretary	n.a.		28.6	(2)	n.a.	
Totals 295	President	23.7	(70)	24.1	(71)	14.2 (41/288)	
	Treasurer/CFO	25.2 (26/103)		35.5 (78/220)		21.7 (64/295)	
	Secretary	66.0 (68/103)		48.2 (106/220)		64.9 (187/288)	

Source: Party records made available to the author.

Notes: Figures in parentheses represent numbers of women.

n.a. = not available.

These data parallel federal figures and suggest that even as baseline increases have occurred in most parties (where the low point of the range is higher in recent years than it was 10 years earlier), the level of female office-holding in riding president and treasurer/CFO jobs continues to be far below that for secretary positions. As one participant pointed out in an interview, "We have far more opportunity now for women to do what used to be the men's jobs in the ridings, but little change in the willingness of men to do what have traditionally been the women's jobs."

Is a party's competitive position related to patterns of female involvement? In the past it was far easier both federally across Canada and provincially within Ontario to identify what constituted a *competitive* political party, meaning a party that held the reins of government or was likely to do so in the near future. Because parties had acknowledged local bases that were marginal, potentially winnable or safe, it was relatively easy to discern patterns by which female activists were clustered in particular types of jobs in specific kinds of ridings. In 1981 in Ontario, for example, two of the three London-area provincial New Democratic Party (NDP) riding associations were headed by women (London at the time was far from fertile NDP territory), as were those in a number of rural Liberal and suburban Progressive Conservative seats. Liberal women were provincial riding presidents in four strong Conservative and two strong NDP ridings. Many women who had broken out of the pink-collar ghetto had done so in ridings where their party was generally inactive and had little chance of electoral success. A substantial number of female riding presidents in all three parties

Table 2.2
Local party participation of women in Ontario, provincial level

Year	President		Treasurer/CFO		Secretary	
	%	N	%	N	%	N
Liberal						
1981	20.0	(25)	29.6	(37)	76.8	(96)
1985	29.6	(37)	39.2	(49)	70.4	(88)
1988	20.0	(26)	23.8	(31)	65.4	(85)
1990	28.5	(37)	26.2	(34)	75.4	(98)
NDP						
1973	8.5	(10)	n.a.		n.a.	
1981	28.8	(36)	41.6	(52)	67.2	(84)
1985	30.4	(38)	36.8	(46)	69.3	(79)b
1988	26.2	(33)a	35.4	(46)	64.8	(70)c
1990	34.6	(45)	29.2	(38)	48.5	(63)
Progressive Conservative						
1977	9.6	(12)	5.6	(7)	62.4	(78)
1981	14.4	(18)	12.0	(15)	66.4	(83)
1985	19.2	(24)	24.0	(30)	69.6	(87)
1988	20.0	(26)	16.9	(22)	62.3	(81)
1990	22.3	(29)	16.9	(22)	64.6	(84)

Source: Figures from 1973 and 1977 are based on internal party studies, while those for
subsequent years are drawn from party records made available to the author.
Notes: Cell entries represent the percentage of local constituency positions held by women in the
years and parties indicated, while figures in parentheses represent the actual number of women
holding these positions. Note that percentages for 1973 are based on a total of 117 provincial
ridings; for 1977, 1981 and 1985 on a total of 125 ridings; and for 1988 and 1990 on a total of
130 ridings.

n.a. = not available.

a Since the position was vacant in 4 ridings, this percentage is calculated on a base of 126.
b Since the position was vacant in some ridings, this percentage is calculated on a base of 114.
c Since the position was vacant in 22 ridings, this percentage is calculated on a base of 108.

seemed to hold symbolic power only, since they had little opportunity
to elect members to their legislative caucus, and thus could not attract
resources from the central provincial organization – which, in turn,
could propel local party activity.

Yet, with the breakdown of traditional Liberal dominance federally and of Progressive Conservative and subsequently Liberal regimes
provincially, it became increasingly difficult to identify whether women
party presidents were clustered in weak or marginal ridings where
their organization had little chance of electoral success. In general, the
distribution of women appears less skewed than in the past, since there
is no longer the very clear concentration of females in president and
CFO positions in marginal constituencies. Part of this change may be

caused by electoral volatility, which makes it difficult for parties to identify their strong versus marginal ridings, and part of it is likely caused by growing demands from party women, and heightened awareness among party élites generally, of the need to give all activists a fair chance at holding local executive positions.

Increases in female participation at the local level may also be attributable to the growth of organized competition for volunteer time, especially interest groups. Some observers have suggested that partisan opportunities for women widened during the 1980s because local gatekeepers could no longer afford to block new talent. If women did not believe that the structure of opportunity in the local party organization was fair, according to this explanation, then there were plenty of other political groups to which they could devote time and effort. This view is particularly relevant to party women who could turn to nonpartisan women's interest groups, in which mobility patterns within the organization were more fluid than in local constituencies with their "pink-collar" sectors.

INTERMEDIATE LEVELS OF ACTIVITY

Three basic types of party work can be considered as intermediate level, bridging the distance between local constituency and élite-level participation. The first of these is convention delegation, where data in table 2.3 indicate growing female participation. The nearly 50 percent

Table 2.3
Women delegates at Canadian party conventions

Party	Year	Women delegates (%)
Federal Progressive Conservative	1967	19.0
Federal Liberal	1968	18.0
Federal NDP	1981	34.7
Federal Progressive Conservative	1981	33.0
Ontario Liberal	1982	39.2
Ontario NDP	1982	40.0
Federal Liberal	1982	37.6
Federal Progressive Conservative	1983 (Winnipeg)	41.4
Federal Progressive Conservative	1983 (Ottawa)	28.0
Federal Progressive Conservative	1989	46.0
Federal Liberal	1990	47.0

Sources: Bashevkin (1985, table 3.3), and party records made available to the author.

figure that had been reached by 1990 in most Canadian parties reflected the longer-term effect of rule changes in those same organizations, modelled in part on the equal representation terms adopted by Democrats in the United States in 1972 (Bashevkin 1985, chap. 4). The means put in place to encourage or require equal numbers of elected male and female party delegates to conventions has varied across parties and jurisdictions, with many of the most extensive and binding regulations operating in the federal and Ontario provincial NDP organizations.

The main problem with these regulations in all parties has been their restriction to directly elected delegates. Ex-officio delegates, especially in the Liberal and Progressive Conservative parties, as well as union delegates in the NDP, have generally not been governed by equal representation rules, and the tendency in the past has been for ex-officio and union delegations to dilute the relatively higher percentage of women in elected party delegations.[2] Party conventions as a whole, therefore, tend to have a lower percentage of women than do directly elected party delegations, a pattern that reflects limits on the significance of directly elected delegates as well as the tendency for women and other groups to fare better in elected than in ex-officio categories.

The second category of intermediate-level involvement concerns federal and provincial party executive positions. As reported in tables 2.4 and 2.5, women in some parties hold a higher percentage of these positions than in earlier years, yet their representation tends to be less than at the level of convention delegation and clearly below that of local constituency secretary. For example, women in 1990 held 38.1 percent of federal Liberal, 58.1 percent of federal New Democratic and 43.1 percent of federal Progressive Conservative party executive positions. In the Ontario provincial parties, the comparable figures were 40.0, 50.0 and 31.3 percent respectively. Table 2.4 reflects the increases

Table 2.4
Federal party office-holding by women in Canada, 1983 and 1990
(percentages)

Party	Organization	1983		1990	
Liberal	National executive	43.3	(13/30)	38.1	(8/21)
	Policy committee	28.6	(6/21)	21.1	(4/19)
NDP	Federal executive	50.0	(6/12)	58.1	(18/31)
	Federal council	60.0	(12/20)	n.a.	
Progressive Conservative	National executive	23.8	(35/147)	43.1	(25/58)

Sources: Bashevkin (1985, table 3.7); and party records made available to the author.

Notes: Figures in parentheses represent the proportion of women holding positions.

n.a. = not available.

Table 2.5
Provincial-level participation by women in Ontario
(percentages)

| Year | Liberal | | NDP | | Progressive Conservative |
	Table officers	Executive committee	Provincial executive	Provincial council	Executive committee
1981	12.5 (1/8)	8.3 (1/12)	39.3 (11/28)	27.9 (41/147)	16.7 (3/18)
1985	37.5 (3/8)	33.3 (8/24)	50.0 (14/28)	34.9 (37/106)	38.9 (7/18)
1988	22.2 (2/9)	34.0 (16/47)[a]	48.3 (15/31)	37.1 (63/170)	28.6 (6/21)
1990	n.a.	40.0 (6/15)	50.0 (15/30)	26.3 (91/346)	31.3 (5/16)

Source: Data are drawn from party records made available to the author.

Notes: Figures in parentheses represent the proportion of women holding positions.
n.a. = not available.

[a] Three positions on the Liberal executive committee were vacant.

that have occurred since 1983 in female office-holding in the federal New Democratic and Conservative parties and the decline in female office-holding during this same period in the federal Liberal party. That is, women constituted 43.3 percent of the members of the federal Liberal executive in 1983 versus 38.1 percent in 1990, and 28.6 percent of the Liberal policy committee in 1983 versus 21.1 percent in 1990. At the provincial level in Ontario, most data in table 2.5 show an increase between 1981 and 1990 in women's participation in party executives.

Cross-party comparisons of these results suggest the effects of affirmative action in both the federal and Ontario New Democratic organizations. Only in the two NDP cases do women obtain and, in the federal case, exceed the 50 percent level in party executive positions. This pattern is consistent with local riding data presented in tables 2.1 and 2.2, which indicate that NDP women have been most likely to break out of the pink-collar sector within constituency organizations and to obtain party president and treasurer/CFO positions.

A third category of intermediate political engagement concerns campaign management. Tables 2.6 through 2.8 summarize data on campaign participation generally, showing that levels of female campaign management tend to vary by party. In the 1988 federal elections, for example, women made up 21.4 percent of Liberal, 30.5 percent of New Democratic and 18.6 percent of Progressive Conservative campaign managers; in the 1990 Ontario provincial elections, comparable figures were 30.8, 37.7 and 23.9 percent respectively.

Table 2.6
Federal campaign participation by Canadian women, 1984 and 1988

	1984 Candidates		1988 Candidates		1988 Campaign managers	
	%	N	%	N	%	N
Liberals	15.2	(43)	17.0	(50)	21.4	(63)
NDP	23.0	(65)	28.8	(85)	30.5	(90)
Progressive Conservatives	8.1	(23)	12.5	(37)	18.6	(55)
Totals	15.5	(131)	19.4	(172)	23.5	(208)

Source: Party records made available to the author.

Table 2.7
Campaign participation of women in Ontario, provincial level, 1981–90

	Liberals			NDP			Progressive Conservatives		
	1981	1987	1990	1981	1987	1990	1981	1987	1990
Candidates	6.4 (8)	20.8 (27)	20.0 (26)	19.2 (24)	35.4 (46)	30.0 (39)	10.4 (13)	16.9 (22)	15.4 (20)
Campaign managers	22.4 (28)	23.8 (31)	30.8 (40)	32.8 (41)	36.9 (48)	37.7 (49)	12.8 (16)	28.5 (37)	23.9 (31)
Total (N)	(36)	(58)	(66)	(65)	(94)	(88)	(29)	(59)	(51)

Source: Data are drawn from Ontario Official Election Returns and from party records.

Notes: Cell entries represent the percentage of women participating; figures in parentheses represent the number. Note that a total of 125 provincial ridings existed in 1981, and 130 in 1987 and 1990.

As in the case of party executive positions, cross-party patterns once again show the highest involvement of women in the NDP and, where comparisons are possible in Ontario, a general increase in the involvement of women in most parties over time. Just as federal party executive data show a decline in women's involvement over time in a long-governing party no longer in office (the federal Liberals), so too do Ontario provincial data on campaign management indicate a decrease in women's involvement in the party which had long ruled the province (the Progressive Conservatives). Taken together, these data point toward fairly consistent increases over time in female numerical representation in the NDP as compared with less consistent and, in some cases, downward patterns of representation in formerly governing parties.

Table 2.8
Campaign participation by women in Ontario by provincial party and
provincial election

		Candidates	Elected MPPs	Placed 2nd	Placed 3rd	Campaign managers
1971	OLP	4	0	0	4	n.a.
	NDP	7	0	3	4	19
	PC	6	2	2	2	n.a.
	Total	17	2	5	10	n.a.
1975	OLP	18	1	8	9	n.a.
	NDP	13	3	2	8	n.a.
	PC	8	3	1	4	n.a.
	Total	39	7	11	21	n.a.
1977	OLP	15	1	8	6	n.a.
	NDP	19	2	5	12	n.a.
	PC	10	3	6	1	9
	Total	44	6	19	19	n.a.
1981	OLP	8	1	5	2	28
	NDP	24	1	1	22	41
	PC	13	4	6	3	16
	Total	45	6	12	27	85
1985	OLP	15	3	8	4	n.a.
	NDP	28	3	6	19	n.a.
	PC	18	3	11	4	n.a.
	Total	61	9	25	27	n.a.
1987	OLP	27	16	11	0	31
	NDP	46	3	16	27	48
	PC	22	1	6	15	37
	Total	95	20	33	42	116
1990	OLP	26	6	18	2	40
	NDP	39	20	13	7	49
	PC	20	3	3	12	31
	Total	85	29	34	21	120

Source: Cell entries for the first four columns are drawn from Ontario Official Election Returns, while figures on campaign management are from party records.

Notes: All cell entries represent the number of women involved. Most data on campaign management other than for the 1981 and 1987 provincial elections were not available. One Conservative candidate in 1990 placed fourth.

n.a. = not available.

One generalization that follows from data on local-level and intermediate-level involvement concerns the rough ordering among parties of female participation. The NDP seems to have the most women engaged at the point of riding president, riding treasurer/CFO, provincial and federal party executive positions and campaign manager, usually followed by the Liberals and Progressive Conservatives in that order. This pattern is helpful to bear in mind as we turn to élite-level involvement, including candidacy for public office, legislative office holding, cabinet appointments and party leadership.[3]

POLITICAL CANDIDACY AND BEYOND

Since the literature on Canadian women and politics has devoted substantial attention to questions of nomination and candidacy, this section places questions of élite participation in the context of party life at all levels (Brodie 1985; Erickson and Carty 1990; Vickers 1978). In this setting, the very pursuit of partisan candidacy, legislative office and other higher positions raises questions about the relationship of feminism to electoral politics. Traditional research on participation describes élite involvement as "gladiatorial," a phrase that evokes images of combat, blood, injury and even death (Milbrath 1965). Such language and imagery have been questioned by scholars who reject a competitive and combative view of politics, arguing that such a perspective is masculine, exclusionary and ultimately not conducive to a humane and cooperative political process (Vickers, 1989, 16–36).

Critical commentary on the use of this language, however, needs to be juxtaposed against the perspectives of women – including feminist women – who participate at élite levels. After seeking nomination for a hotly contested urban seat, one candidate with a history of women's movement involvement reflected, "Politics at that élite level really is a blood sport. Unlike at the local riding or party executive level, there simply are no consolation prizes. People go for the jugular to get nominated in a winnable seat; I'm afraid that's the reality."

This disparity between feminist prescriptions for consensual and humane politics, on the one hand, and the highly competitive and, at times, combative reality of élite party involvement, on the other, reflects a long-standing problem for Canadian women. Captured in the dilemma between partisanship and political independence that faced the early Canadian women's movement, feminists during the 1990s are confronted with a parallel set of challenges to their beliefs at the peak of mainstream party organizations.[4]

In empirical terms, the growing involvement of women as major party candidates during the past decade is reflected in tables 2.6 through 2.8. The total number of federal candidates increased from 131 or 15.5 percent in 1984 to 172 or 19.4 percent in 1988. At the provincial level in

Ontario, 85 women candidates (21.8 percent) contested office for the three major parties in 1990 compared with 45 (12.0 percent) in 1981.

One major criticism of the candidacy situation is that female nominees at both federal and provincial levels tend to run in ridings where their parties are not in a competitive position. The tendency for parties to nominate women in constituencies held by the leader of another party, or in other presumably marginal seats, has been viewed as evidence that women face considerable hurdles at the élite level. It is argued, in short, that few women run in their parties' competitive constituencies where political stakes are high.

In part as a reaction to this criticism, some political parties have made a conscious decision to field more women candidates in competitive seats, even if fewer female candidates are nominated in total. Such a decline can be attributed to a qualitative as opposed to quantitative approach to candidacy; fewer women are fielded overall but the ridings in which they do run are more politically promising than in the past. In 1990 in Ontario, for example, the provincial NDP purposefully ran women in all three Metropolitan Toronto seats that had been vacated by NDP incumbents; overall, the party fielded fewer female candidates in 1990 (39 or 30.0 percent) than it had in 1987 (46 or 35.4 percent).[5]

This conscious decision, together with a history in the NDP of running relatively large numbers of women and a major electoral shift in the province, produced obvious legislative results: in 1990, the Ontario NDP elected 20 women MPPs as compared with only 3 in 1987. The NDP government caucus at Queen's Park included 27.0 percent women (20 out of 74) and the 1990 Ontario cabinet included 11 female ministers out of 26 members (42.3 percent). Much like previous increases in élite-level participation, these record numbers in Ontario may create new thresholds, new benchmarks against which future provincial and federal governments are measured.

Major electoral shifts also produced substantial change in women's representation at the federal level. The 1984 Progressive Conservative landslide helped to elect many women in areas that had traditionally been considered weak for that party, including the province of Quebec, and meant that the number of female MPs nearly doubled from 14 (5.0 percent) in 1980 to 27 (9.6 percent) in 1984. This level increased once again to 39 (13.2 percent) in 1988.

Increased participation can also be seen in data on cabinet office and party leadership. Unlike the situation that prevailed in the 1960s when one woman was seen as a maximum limit within federal cabinets, 1990 figures show 6 out of 36 (16.7 percent) women in the federal cabinet. This quantitative shift has been accompanied by a qualitative one as well, where female ministers after the mid-1980s were appointed to senior justice and economic portfolios rather than strictly to health, education, status of women and other less prestigious departments.

Finally, some changes have occurred at the level of party leadership. In the past, women obtained party leadership in organizations that did not hold the reins of power at the time and were viewed as unlikely to become the governing party in the near future. Typified by the case of Thérèse Casgrain, who headed the Quebec Co-operative Commonwealth Federation (CCF) during the 1950s, Canadian women have led a host of relatively uncompetitive provincial parties, including the British Columbia Liberals, Nova Scotia New Democrats and New Brunswick Progressive Conservatives.[6]

In a number of instances, women have won the leadership of a party that, at the time of their selection, was not in a competitive position, but that, under their leadership, obtained a more competitive position. At the provincial level, the example of Sharon Carstairs is illustrative: the Manitoba Liberals were in a weak position when Carstairs was selected as provincial leader but subsequently obtained official opposition status from 1988 to 1990. At the federal level, Audrey McLaughlin won the leadership of the New Democratic Party in 1989, when the party was relatively low in the polls. The NDP went on to improve its standing in national public opinion surveys.

Women have increasingly broken out of this mould to contest the leadership of competitive parties. For example, Flora MacDonald ran in 1976 for the leadership of the federal Progressive Conservatives, Muriel Smith in 1979 for the Manitoba NDP, Grace McCarthy and Kim Campbell in 1986 for the British Columbia Social Credit party, and Sheila Copps in 1982 and 1990 for the Ontario and federal Liberal parties, respectively. In each instance, these campaigns have been unsuccessful in the sense that the candidates lost but successful to the extent that women's claims to competitive party leadership were taken more seriously (Bashevkin 1985, 89–97).

CONFRONTING THE BARRIERS

Efforts to increase the number of women engaged in Canadian party politics have encountered many of the problems discussed in previous work in this field (Bashevkin 1985, chap. 1; Brodie 1985). Limitations related to the systematic tracking of women away from élite-level party work have been challenged in a number of ways in recent years. First, beginning with the establishment in 1972 of a Toronto group known as Women for Political Action, many grassroots women's organizations have been established across the country to pressure for more numbers –

especially in federal and provincial legislatures. Led for the most part by liberal feminists, some of whom have been party activists and some of whom have been nonpartisan, these women and politics groups have sponsored seminars, books, press conferences, television programs, symposia, legislative internships, skills-training workshops and other activities designed to elect more women.[7]

Second, proposals have been made to institute structural changes in the broader political process, usually by these same women and politics groups. The Committee for '94 in Toronto, for example, was established in 1984 with the goal of electing women to half the seats in the House of Commons by 1994. In studying, and in the case of some members, experiencing the difficulties involved in reaching this goal, the Committee developed a policy statement advocating reform of electoral finance laws. It pressured for complete public funding of nomination contests, elections and party leadership campaigns, arguing that the present system of tax credits for election contributions makes it difficult for women and other disadvantaged groups to raise money and hence hold public office (Committee for '94, 1990).

Third, attempts have been made by the political parties to institute formal and informal reforms. At the level of constitutional change, for example, some federal and provincial parties have adopted rules that specify equal proportions of male and female constituency delegates to conventions and that encourage similar provisions for legislative candidates and local riding association executives (Bashevkin 1985, chap. 4). As well, some parties have worked actively to recruit women as candidates for party and public office, and have offered campaign schools designed to attract and train these candidates.

Many of these internal reforms represent a response to pressures from party women's organizations. As summarized in earlier work, the federal Liberal and Progressive Conservative parties had modernized their older auxiliary-style women's associations by the early 1980s, while the federal NDP (which never established a traditional women's association) created a Participation of Women (POW) Committee in 1969 (Bashevkin 1985, chap. 5). Party women's organizations have also been instrumental in establishing special funds to assist female candidates. The Judy LaMarsh Fund in the federal Liberal organization, the Agnes MacPhail Fund in the federal NDP and the Ellen Fairclough Foundation created by the federal Progressive Conservatives each represent a fund-raising priority for activists in their organizations.

Yet, questions have been raised in all three parties about the influence of internal groups. According to some observers, women would best devote their energies to mainstream party work in local ridings and to party executives rather than to "hiving themselves off" in separate party women's groups. This argument has been advanced by some partisans who maintain that the mainstream organizational opportunities for women have never been more promising. According to a different line of argument, however, party women's organizations are necessary because they continue to provide a supportive environment for women's efforts and play a crucial role in monitoring women's progress at all levels of party life.

One area in which party women's groups have made an important contribution, even according to their critics, is in the matter of nominations. Most academic as well as internal party accounts of female participation highlight the problem of entry to élite-level politics. Particularly in the Liberal and Progressive Conservative federal organizations, where competing for a winnable urban nomination can cost more than $100 000, party women's organizations have drawn attention to enormous inequalities between male and female access. If women in the labour force generally earn less than 70 cents for every dollar earned by a man, then the individual financial resources they bring to contested nominations are also considerably less. Male candidates have traditionally come from the fields of law and business, where average earnings and fund-raising connections are far more lucrative than in the fields from which many female candidates emerge, notably social work, journalism and education.

Since Revenue Canada data show that women are less likely to contribute to campaigns and that, when they do contribute, they donate fewer dollars on average than men, then the financial obstacles to female candidacy loom even larger.[8] According to one activist who initially claimed there was little use for the women's organization in her party, "I give that women's group credit because they have convinced people that the nominations issue is important. This is crucial and it leads me to think that maybe the [women's organization] does do useful work."

A somewhat different set of concerns about underrepresentation follows from research on media coverage of women in Canadian politics. Particularly at the point of nomination for major party leadership, women candidates tend to become the focus of highly personalized, style-oriented press coverage (Bashevkin 1985, 89–92). Sometimes in response to this phenomenon, packagers, pollsters and other presumed experts on electoral politics may try to "manage" female candidates in a way that minimizes the distinctiveness – including the feminist content – of the candidates' policies, thus homogenizing or standardizing the nominee. As a former federal party president and candidate reflected on this situation, "The real power in the parties is in the hands of the strategists, polling experts and consultants, almost all of whom are men. Women have to take their advice, at least until we can come up with some alternative ways to do élite politics."

COMPARATIVE PERSPECTIVES

Reflecting on the number of women who are active in Canadian party politics sometimes leads to predictable and depressing conclusions. Yes, the analyst concludes, more women now hold local party president and treasurer/CFO positions, but look at how many remain in a pink-collar ghetto in local ridings. Yes, more women hold federal and provincial party executive positions and serve as convention delegates, campaign managers and candidates, but see how few win election to provincial and federal legislatures. Élite cabinet positions are only rarely held by women, and no Canadian woman has yet won the leadership of a competitive political party.

Depressing and predictable as this perspective may be, it conceals a set of figures that in comparative terms are relatively exciting and unpredictable. Among advanced liberal democracies, which share single-member plurality arrangements, federal systems or parliamentary traditions, Canada hardly constitutes a representational backwater for women. Research by Joni Lovenduski (1990) of Loughborough University, for example, reports that women made up only 6.6 percent of Conservative and 15.0 percent of Labour candidates in the 1987 British elections, after which Prime Minister Margaret Thatcher appointed no women to her cabinet. According to Lovenduski, both major parties in the United Kingdom continue to exclude women candidates from their regional strongholds, Labour in the north and Conservatives in the south.

Studies of the United States and Australia also suggest that participation in Canada is relatively high. According to a conference paper by Melissa Haussman (1990) of Duke University, women hold only 5 percent of seats in the U.S. Congress and 17 percent of seats in U.S. state legislatures. A national total of 59 women obtained party nomination to run for the House of Representatives in 1988 compared with 22 in 1982. Similarly, data on election to the Australian House of Representatives compiled by Colin Hughes (1990) of the University of Queensland suggest that "little has changed. The major parties [in 1990] were still hurling the majority of their women candidates against the most heavily fortified of their enemy's seats."[9]

In short, many of the limitations affecting women's party participation in Canada are not country-specific and can be identified in most comparable political systems. Moreover, much of the focus in Canada on reforming the nomination process and ensuring that women activists at all levels are not confined to uncompetitive party environments is receiving attention elsewhere as well. As in Canada, this reform process has tended to take root initially in parties of the left, followed by those of the centre, and then those on the right.

It seems that internal party reform is critical to increasing both the quantity and quality of women's political engagement in all of these systems. Yet, electoral volatility along with the growing attractiveness of interest groups as alternatives to parties have themselves produced major improvements in women's political representation in Canada. In fact, fickle behaviour on the part of Canadian voters during the mid-1980s and following years tended to weaken the effectiveness of many long-standing and highly discriminatory party practices vis-à-vis women. For example, if parties no longer know where their safe versus weak seats are, then they are hard pressed to channel women as local party presidents or candidates into marginal ridings.

In conclusion, the kinds of reforms proposed by organizations inside and outside the major parties may help to improve not only women's representation, but also that of other historically marginal groups. Opening up systems of party nomination, challenging the dominant role of money in party life, and questioning the "packaging" of élites can all help to widen the recruitment base of party organizations and can make them more attractive to people with diverse identities. By moving parties toward internal reform, women have begun to construct an élite that is no longer exclusively white, male and middle-class. The logical extension of this process would attract Aboriginal, ethnic and visible minority activists to a more representative Canadian party system.

NOTES

Prepared for Symposium on the Active Participation of Women in Politics, Royal Commission on Electoral Reform and Party Financing, l'École Polytechnique de Montréal, 1 November 1990.

I am grateful to Karen Jones for research assistance in the preparation of this paper, and to Cynthia Cusinato, Mary McGowan, Joan Kouri and Marian Maloney of the Liberal party; Ed Dale, Deanna Beach, Abby Pollonetsky and Jill Marzetti of the New Democratic Party; and Suzanne Warren, Mary Meldrum, Catherine Mustard, Margaret Steeves, Barbara Colantonio and Joe Morrow of the Progressive Conservative party for providing data on their organizations. My thanks as well to the three anonymous assessors who reviewed an earlier version of this paper for the Royal Commission.

1. Ontario provincial data are introduced in this study to try to supplement federal-level figures. Given the difficulty of collecting federal data and the inevitable gaps in the national results which are reported, Ontario figures are used as a basis of comparison. Ontario has three major provincial parties, largely mirroring the federal party system in a historic sense, and has been the subject of sustained empirical attention. It should be noted, however, that women's involvement at the provincial level in Ontario has tended to be more extensive than in other provincial party systems in Canada (Bashevkin et al. 1990, 293–310; Bashevkin and Holder 1985, 275–87).

2. For data on this, see Bashevkin (1985, 63–64).

3. On the hierarchy of political involvement, see Milbrath (1965).

4. For the terms of this historic dilemma, see Bashevkin (1985, chap. 1).

5. These ridings were Scarborough West, vacated by Richard Johnston; Riverdale, vacated by David Reville; and Beaches–Woodbine, vacated by Marion Bryden.

6. Other provincial parties which have been led by women include the Saskatchewan Liberals and New Brunswick New Democrats.

7. Although these groups have adopted different names across the country, they developed a communications network that connects, for example, the 52% Solution based in Atlantic Canada, Femmes regroupées pour l'accessibilité aux pouvoirs politiques et économiques (FRAPPE) in Montreal, the Committee for '94 in Toronto and Winning Women in Vancouver. Materials that have been produced include Josephine Payne-O'Connor's *Sharing Power: A Political Skills Handbook* (1986) and a six-part television series by TVOntario based on a 1986 conference organized by the Committee for '94.

8. According to data from the Statistical Services Division of Revenue Canada Taxation, fewer women claimed political contribution tax credits and, on average, women contributed fewer dollars than men in the 1980 through 1987 tax years. I am grateful to Lisa Young of the Royal Commission on Electoral Reform and Party Financing for these data.

9. Parallel conclusions are reached in Simms (1990).

REFERENCES

Bashevkin, Sylvia B. 1985. *Toeing the Lines: Women and Party Politics in English Canada*. Toronto: University of Toronto Press.

Bashevkin, Sylvia, and Marianne Holder. 1985. "The Politics of Female Participation." In *The Government and Politics of Ontario*. 3d ed., ed. Donald C. MacDonald. Scarborough: Nelson Canada.

Bashevkin, Sylvia, Marianne Holder and Karen Jones. 1990. "Women's Political Involvement and Policy Influence." In *The Government and*

Politics of Ontario. 4th ed., ed. Graham White. Scarborough: Nelson Canada.

Brodie, Janine. 1985. *Women and Politics in Canada.* Toronto: McGraw-Hill Ryerson.

Committee for '94. 1990. "Let Women Play Too! The Case for Public Funding of Canadian Elections." Brief presented to the Royal Commission on Electoral Reform and Party Financing, 7 May. Toronto: The Committee.

Erickson, Lynda, and R.K. Carty. 1990. "Candidate Selection in Canadian Political Parties." Paper presented at the American Political Science Association meetings held in San Francisco.

Haussman, Melissa. 1990. "Party Workhorses but not Party Animals: American and Canadian Women in Political Party Organizations." Paper presented at the American Political Science Association meetings held in San Francisco.

Hughes, Colin A. 1990. "A Target Missed: Women in Australian Elections." Paper presented at the American Political Science Association meetings held in San Francisco.

LaMarsh, Judy. 1969. *Memoirs of a Bird in a Gilded Cage.* Toronto: McClelland and Stewart.

Lovenduski, Joni. 1990. "Women and Politics Worldwide, U.K." Paper presented at the American Political Science Association meetings held in San Francisco. Forthcoming in *Women and Politics Worldwide,* ed. Barbara J. Nelson and Najma Chowdury. New Haven: Yale University Press.

Milbrath, Lester. 1965. *Political Participation.* Chicago: Rand McNally.

Mishler, William. 1979. *Political Participation in Canada.* Toronto: Macmillan.

Payne-O'Connor, Josephine. 1986. *Sharing Power: A Political Skills Handbook.* Victoria: Kachina Press.

Simms, Marian. 1990. "Candidate Selection in Australia." Paper presented at the American Political Science Association meetings held in San Francisco.

Vickers, Jill McCalla. 1978. "Where Are the Women in Canadian Politics?" *Atlantis* 3 (Spring): 40–51.

––––––. 1989. "Feminist Approaches to Women in Politics." In *Beyond the Vote: Canadian Women and Politics,* ed. Linda Kealey and Joan Sangster. Toronto: University of Toronto Press.

3

LEGISLATIVE TURNOVER AND THE ELECTION OF WOMEN TO THE CANADIAN HOUSE OF COMMONS

Lisa Young

ALTHOUGH CANADIAN WOMEN have had the right to vote and run for federal office for the past 70 years, they remain seriously under-represented in the House of Commons. The number of women elected has increased in each general election, but the rate of change remains slow; at present, only 13.5 percent of the members of the House of Commons are women. Even at that relatively low level, the proportion of women in the House is greater than the proportion in the lower houses of the United States, the United Kingdom, France and Australia – all at 6 percent. Among Western nations with single-member plural-ity electoral systems, Canada lags behind only New Zealand, where 14.4 percent of the members of the lower house are women (Inter-Parliamentary Union 1988).

No one factor determines the number of women elected in Canada and elsewhere. Rather, a number of factors – including the political sys-tem and electoral laws, the status of women in society, media images of female politicians, political party attitudes and policies, and acces-sibility of financial, human and other resources – contribute to the per-sistent under-representation of women in politics.[1] Frequently cited as a barrier to the election of women is the availability of seats in the leg-islature (that is, the low turnover rate of the legislature's membership).

Essentially, this argument states that the rate at which the mem-bership of the legislature changes (through voluntary retirement and defeat of incumbents) affects or determines the rate at which women can enter the legislature. Although there is ample evidence to suggest that a low turnover rate is a serious barrier to the election of women to the American Congress, it is less clear that this is the case in Canada. The purpose of this study is to examine the applicability of this proposition to the Canadian situation and to consider whether the availability of seats is an opportunity or a barrier to women seeking public office in Canada. To examine this proposition, a model of legislative turnover developed by American scholars is adapted to the Canadian case.

THE ELECTION OF WOMEN IN CANADA

Before examining the effects of vacancy and incumbency rates on the election of women in Canada, it is important to understand the pattern of candidacy and election of women. As is demonstrated in table 3.1, there is a persistent disparity between the percentage of candidates who are women and the percentage of elected members who are women. Stated otherwise, female candidates are less likely to win than are male candidates (see table 3.2). From 20 percent to 24 percent of female candidates were elected in the elections of 1980, 1984 and 1988, while 34–36 percent of male candidates were elected. This disparity suggests, in

Table 3.1
Women: Candidates and elected, general elections of 1980, 1984 and 1988

Year	Party	Female candidates (N)	Female candidates as percentage of all candidates	Women elected (N)	Women elected as percentage of all elected
1980	Liberal	23	8.2	12	8.0
	Progressive Conservative	14	5.0	2	1.9
	New Democratic Party	32	11.0	2	6.0
	Total	69	8.0	16	5.0
1984	Liberal	45	16.0	5	12.5
	Progressive Conservative	23	8.2	19	9.0
	New Democratic Party	64	22.7	4	13.3
	Total	132	15.6	28	9.9
1988	Liberal	51	17.3	13	15.7
	Progressive Conservative	37	12.5	21	12.4
	New Democratic Party	84	28.5	5	11.6
	Total	172	19.4	39	13.2

Sources: Bashevkin (1985, 73); Brodie (1985, 4); and election results published in *Canadian News Facts* 18:16 (19 Sept. 1984) and 23:21 (4 Dec. 1988).

Table 3.2
Percentage of male and female candidates elected in 1980, 1984 and 1988 general elections

Year	Party	Percentage of female candidates elected (a)	Percentage of male candidates elected (b)	Differential (male–female) (b - a)
1980	Liberal	52	52	0
	Progressive Conservative	14	38	24
	New Democratic Party	6	12	6
	Total	23	34	11
1984	Liberal	9	15	6
	Progressive Conservative	83	74	-9
	New Democratic Party	6	12	6
	Total	20	36	16
1988	Liberal	26	29	3
	Progressive Conservative	57	57	0
	New Democratic Party	6	18	12
	Total	23	36	13

Sources: Bashevkin (1985, 73); Brodie (1985, 4); and election results published in Canadian News Facts 18:16 (19 Sept. 1984) and 23:21 (4 Dec. 1988).

Notes: The percentage of female/male candidates elected is calculated by dividing the number of women/men elected by the number of women/men who ran (expressed as a percentage). The differential is calculated by subtracting the percentage of female candidates elected from the percentage of male candidates elected.

turn, the existence of bias against women, most likely in the form of nominating female candidates primarily in "unwinnable" ridings.

There are, however, notable exceptions to the pattern outlined above. Specifically, the disparity between the percentage of candidates who are women and the percentage of elected members who are women was not present for the winning party in any of the three elections under consideration. As table 3.2 demonstrates, although male candidates *overall* are more likely than female candidates to win their seat, the same is not true for candidates of the winning party.

At first glance, this pattern negates the conventional explanation of why women are entering the House of Commons at such a low rate. If women are nominated primarily by minor parties in hopeless ridings, why are women candidates for the winning party as likely, or more likely, to win than their male counterparts?

It is probable that many of these women are winning unexpectedly – they were intended as "sacrifice" candidates, but were swept up on the tide of their party's electoral success. Notably, in 1984, 10 of the Progressive Conservative (PC) party's 14 new female MPs were elected in Quebec, where the Conservative party had been a minor party for two decades, holding only one seat in the previous Parliament. Because of the Conservative party's prior weakness in Quebec, it can be surmised that competition for candidacies was less intense than in traditional strongholds and that the pool of qualified potential candidates was more limited than it would have been for a party with a strong traditional base in the province. Given that the Conservative party was essentially a minor party in Quebec before the 1984 election, the conventional understanding applies.

This explanation, however, does not apply to the elections of 1980 and 1988. In neither case did the winning party gain a large number of seats in a region where it was previously weak. In 1980, most of the women who ran for the Liberal party were incumbents, and the rate of incumbency for women in that election was extremely high (92 percent). In 1988, women running under the PC banner not only had a slightly higher success rate than their male counterparts, but also represented a considerably larger proportion of the candidates than they had in 1984. This suggests that the parties may have made a conscious effort to increase the number of female MPs: the number of women in the Conservative caucus increased by two, even though the caucus itself was considerably smaller after the 1988 election.

The results of the 1988 election suggest that a new dynamic might be emerging. The Conservative party, which until 1984 had had an extremely poor track record in electing women, appears to be consolidating the vast increase in the number of women in its Parliamentary caucus through a deliberate attempt to nominate women in "winnable" ridings. Alternatively, it is possible that female members of the Liberal and PC parties are aware of the tendency to recruit women to run in unwinnable ridings and are, consequently, increasingly unwilling to serve as candidates in these ridings.

The New Democratic Party (NDP), on the other hand, has for many years pursued the goal of increasing to 50 percent the percentage of candidates who are female. The result has been the disproportionate nomination of women in unwinnable ridings. As table 3.2 shows, the differential between the success rate for female candidates and male candidates decreased dramatically for the Conservative party; remained more or less constant for the Liberals; and, for the NDP, increased from 6 percentage points in 1980 to 12 percentage points in 1988.

While it is evident that there is still bias against female candidates (women are more likely than men to be nominated in an unwinnable riding), this bias has decreased somewhat in recent years, particularly in the PC and Liberal parties. This suggests that there are two reasons for the small number of women elected: some degree of bias against women in the recruitment and nomination process, and a limited supply of women willing to run.

There are three possible routes into the House of Commons: through re-election, by defeating an incumbent member, or by winning an open seat (a seat where there is no incumbent MP running). In recent elections, there has been little difference between incumbency rates for men and for women.[2] This means that women do not have any particular advantage or disadvantage when running again. Once elected, their seats are no safer or more marginal than those of their male counterparts. Similarly, women are no less able to unseat incumbents than are men.[3]

The evidence concerning women's access to open seats is inconclusive (see table 3.3). Except for the NDP in 1988, the proportion of women running in open seats was equal to or greater than the proportion of candidates who were women for each party. Moreover, the same is true for candidates elected who were women. These numbers suggest that for both the PCs and the Liberals, open seats are an important point of entry for women. The figures for the Liberals suggest that winnable open seats are targeted for women. Open seats are a relatively important entry point for women into the system. It follows, then, that the availability of open seats affects the opportunities for women to be elected.

Table 3.3
Women's access to open seats

General election	Party	Candidates (women as percentage of all candidates in open seats)	Elected (women as percentage of all candidates elected in open seats)
1984	Liberal	18	30
	Progressive Conservative	11	10
	New Democratic Party	27	20
	Total	13	14
1988	Liberal	17	29
	Progressive Conservative	22	17
	New Democratic Party	23	11
	Total	21	18

Source: Canadian News Facts 18:16 (19 September 1984) and 23:21 (4 December 1988).

Note: The 1980 election was excluded from this table because there were very few open seats.

THE EFFECT OF VACANCY AND INCUMBENCY
ON THE ELECTION OF WOMEN

When considering the integration of an under-represented societal group (such as women or visible minorities) into an elected body, it is important to take into account the effect that the rate of legislative turnover can have on the rate of increase in the number of group members elected. Simply put, if the membership of the legislature changes very slowly, then the ethnic or gender composition of the legislature will necessarily change slowly. There are two elements of legislative turnover: voluntary vacancies (members of Parliament who choose not to run again) and defeated incumbents (members of Parliament who choose to run again but lose the election to a challenger).

The effect of legislative turnover and incumbency rates on the number of women elected has been the subject of considerable academic attention in the United States. This is no doubt a reflection of the extremely low turnover rate in the American House of Representatives as well as the powerful incumbency advantage that characterizes American congressional elections (see Cain et al. 1987). Darcy, Welsh and Clark (1987, 150–51) observe that the low turnover rate in the House of Representatives means there are few newcomers after any congressional election. As a result, there is little opportunity for women's representation in the House to increase. While the number of women candidates is increasing, they tend to be unsuccessful because they are contesting seats in which there is an incumbent. The authors conclude that it is the power of incumbency, not discrimination against women, that prevents a more rapid increase in the number of women in the House of Representatives. The authors also observe that women are entering state legislatures at a considerably higher rate than they are the national legislature, and they suggest that this is a consequence of a higher turnover rate in state legislatures.

In a similar vein, Susan Carroll (1985, 106) has concluded that the effect of incumbency and the low number of open seats are powerful explanations for why women have been so unsuccessful in American elections at the state and the national level. Moreover, in a study of the determinants of the election of women to state legislatures, Carol Nechemias (1987, 135) found that every 10 percent increase in the rate of legislative turnover increases the proportion of women legislators by 2.74 percent. Vallance and Davies (1986) note that one of the probable explanations for the considerable number of women elected to the European Parliament in 1979 (the first direct Euro-election) was that there were no incumbents to overcome. The unprecedented number of legislative vacancies provided an opportunity for women that resulted in a legislature whose membership was 16 percent female, a sharp contrast to the average of 9 percent in the national legislatures of the European Community member states at that time.

Darcy and Choike (1986) have developed a model to explain the relationship between legislative turnover and the number of women elected. This model suggests that, in the absence of bias (positive or negative) toward women candidates, the proportion of women in the legislature will eventually stabilize at the proportion of new candidates who are women. In other words, the proportion of elected members who are women will be equal to the proportion of candidates who are women. Incumbency, however, delays this process. As a consequence, the greater the rate of incumbency, the longer it will be until this stabilization takes place. Assuming a relatively high incumbency rate, the legislative turnover rate acts as a constraint on the rate of increase of women in the legislature.

The American experience is not directly applicable to the Canadian situation. In any given election, approximately 90 percent of the members of the House of Representatives run again, and more than 90 percent of those who do run will win. Low vacancy and incumbency, therefore, present a serious constraint to rapid change in the composition of that legislature. In table 3.4, however, we see that in Canadian elections an average of 16 percent of members of Parliament do not run again, and 20 percent of those who do run are not re-elected

Table 3.4
Retirement and incumbency rates, House of Commons, 1980–88

General election	Voluntary vacancies (N)	Members defeated (N)	New members (as percentage of all MPs)
1968	52	53	28
1972	49	58	41
1974	17	39	21
1979*	60	45	44
1980	12	42	19
1984	56	88	51
1988*	59	62	45

Source: Docherty (1990b).
*Size of House increased by 18 in 1979 and by 13 in 1988.

(Franks 1987, 74). The constraints imposed by low vacancy and incumbency are much less serious in Canada than in the United States.

The Canadian electoral system, in contrast to the American, places greater emphasis on the candidates' party affiliation than on the candidates themselves (see Clarke et al. 1991).[4] The past 30 years have seen the emergence of a strong "personal vote"– a tendency among voters to base voting decisions on the characteristics of the incumbent candidate rather than on the party or the issues – in both the United States and, to a lesser degree, the United Kingdom. Research suggests, however, that there has been no similar development in Canada (Ferejohn and Gaines 1991). The advantage of incumbency is, therefore, much less powerful in the Canadian context.

It is notable that in both the 1984 and 1988 elections, the increase in the number of women in the House of Commons was experienced primarily by the party that gained the most seats relative to its previous standing. Specifically, in 1984, the Conservative landslide included 19 women, a substantial increase from the 2 women in the PC caucus before the election. While women made up only 1.9 percent of the PC caucus after the 1980 election, they made up 9 percent of the caucus after the 1984 ballot. Similarly, when the Liberal party won several seats in 1988 at the expense of the Conservative party, the number of women in the Liberal caucus increased from 4 to 13, or from 10 percent of the caucus to 15.7 percent.

The Model

To demonstrate more clearly the effect of turnover rates on the opportunities for women, the model developed by Darcy and Choike, and operationalized by Darcy, Welsh and Clark has been modified to reflect the Canadian situation and to compare the opportunities for women under the assumption of Canadian and American turnover rates.

The model reflects the three entry patterns discussed above: re-election, defeating an incumbent, and winning an open seat. Parameters of the model reflect the legislative turnover rate, the systemic bias either for or against women and the proportion of new candidates who are women. By substituting different values for these parameters, reflecting different possible future trends, it is possible to assess the impact of various factors on the election of women.

The model projects the proportion of men and women in the new legislature based on the proportion of women and men in the old legislature, estimations of the return rate for women and for men (which tend to be almost identical in Canada), and assumptions regarding bias for or against women and the proportion of new candidates who will

Figure 3.1
Model of legislative turnover

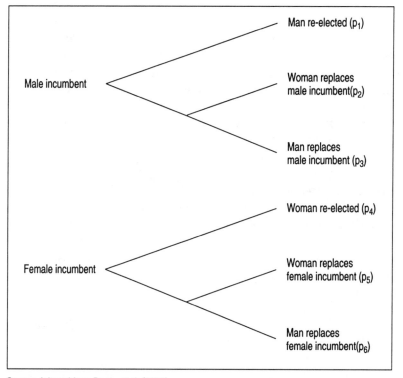

Source: Adaped from Darcy et al. (1987).

be women. This projection then feeds back into the model as the proportion of women and men in the old legislature for the subsequent election. In the case of a male incumbent, there are three possible outcomes: he may be re-elected, defeated by a male challenger or defeated by a female challenger. Similarly, in the case of a female incumbent, there are also three possible outcomes: she may be re-elected, defeated by a male challenger or defeated by a female challenger[5] (see figure 3.1).

The dynamics of the model are relatively simple. The model assumes that male incumbents will be replaced by women gradually as men retire and are defeated in general elections. As a consequence, the lower the rate of legislative turnover – the greater the rate of return – the slower the rate of increase in the proportion of women in the legislature. The greater the percentage of new candidates (nonincumbents) who are women, the greater will be the proportion of women in the new legislature. In addition, bias against women (measured as the difference between women as a proportion of all candidates and women as a proportion of all elected MPs) slows the rate of increase, while bias in favour of women hastens it.

The value of the model lies in its ability to demonstrate the impact of the turnover rate on the rate at which the number of women in the House increases. Holding all other parameters constant, the model allows comparison of the effects of high and low turnover rates as represented by the Canadian and American cases. The model is also useful in demonstrating the impact of other elements of the opportunity structure, specifically systemic bias that advantages or disadvantages women, as well as the percentage of new candidates who are women. By changing the values of these parameters, it is possible to assess the effect of an increase in the number of female candidates or a decrease in the systemic bias against women noted earlier in this study.

The model is not, however, a predictive device because there is no way to determine the values for many of the parameters of the model with complete accuracy; it is also impossible to predict significant changes to these parameters that may occur. The determinants of the value of the proportion of female candidates and the bias against women include such disparate and intangible factors as political culture, societal values, attitudes of party élites and selectorates, and the availability of "qualified" candidates. Many of these determinants – most notably political culture and societal values – have undergone considerable change in the past quarter-century and, to some extent, are still in flux. There is consequently no "scientific" basis upon which a researcher can make credible predictions of the future values of the parameters of the model. It is only possible to identify possible future scenarios and to project the effects of such scenarios on the election of women. It must be stressed that the model is a heuristic, and not a predictive, device.

Moreover, the model does not take into consideration the Canadian party system and, therefore, will not give an entirely accurate picture of the effects of changes in these parameters. Specifically, because bias in the system is measured as the difference between the percentage of candidates who are women and the percentage of elected members who are women, the aggregate measure of bias is not an accurate depiction of the actual relationship. In fact, the measure of bias differs considerably for the different parties. Because the model does not lend itself to modification to account for differing degrees of bias among the three major parties, the aggregate measure must be used as a proxy. It should also be noted that the model does not take into account the unexpected wins that tend to lead to the greatest increase in the number of women elected. Consequently, it reflects static rather than dynamic assumptions about the election of women and, therefore, does not capture the full extent of the upward trend in the number of women elected in recent elections. Despite this, the model does remain the best empirical tool available for exploring the impact of the turnover rate and changes in the values of the parameters.

The Results

The model has been run using various assumptions. In all cases, the initial situation is the current one (13.2 percent of MPs are women). Return rates were calculated by taking an average of the return rates for women and men in the 1984 and 1988 elections. An average of these two elections was used because the 1984 election resulted in a change of government and an extremely high turnover, while the 1988 election had less dramatic results. Because the Canadian system tends to alternate irregularly between elections with high and moderate turnover, the 1984 and 1988 elections are good indicators of average return rates.

Six scenarios were developed to represent possible future trends. The first scenario represents a "worst case" in which there is absolutely no progress from the current situation. Women remain at 17.8 percent of all new candidates (as in the 1988 election) and the current bias against women remains. This bias is estimated at 6 percent, which is the difference between the percentage of candidates who are women and the percentage of elected members who are women. Again, this reflects the situation in the 1988 election. As table 3.5 demonstrates, this would result in virtually no increase in the number of women elected in the foreseeable future.

In the second scenario, women remain at 17.8 percent of all new candidates, but the bias against women is removed. This represents a situation in which women are just as likely to win as are men or, in other words, a situation in which women are no more likely to be nominated in hopeless ridings than are men. This scenario would yield only marginal gains in the proportion of women in the House.

In the third scenario, the negative bias against women remains, while the proportion of new candidates who are women increases by three percentage points each election. This scenario yields greater gains in the representation of women than does the second scenario, in which there is no bias, but the proportion of women among new candidates remains constant.

The fourth scenario reflects a situation in which there is no bias against women candidates (as was the case in the second scenario) and the percentage of new candidates who are women increases by three percentage points each election. Such a scenario would result in a considerable increase in the percentage of women in the House – to almost 33 percent within five elections.

The fifth scenario presents a more optimistic picture. The percentage of candidates who are women increases by three percentage points each election, and there is a 3 percent bias in favour of women. For such a situation to come about, there would have to be a conscious attempt by political parties to place women in strategic ridings. This scenario would yield substantial increases in women's representation in the House.

The sixth scenario, or "best case," assumes that the proportion of candidates who are women increases by five percentage points each election and that there is a considerable (6 percent) bias in favour of women. To put this into perspective, the positive bias that is being assumed in this case is equal to the negative bias that was present in the 1988 election. Again, for such a scenario to come about, it would be necessary for political parties to make a serious commitment to recruiting women as candidates and placing them in ridings that are likely to yield victory. This scenario would bring the percentage of women in the House close to 50 percent within five elections (see table 3.5 and figure 3.2).

The model was also run using all of the same parameters and assumptions, but American return rates were substituted for Canadian return rates. The results (see table 3.6) reflect the impact that a low legislative turnover rate has on the prospects for the election of women.

What, then, do these projections explain about the election of women? One of the more striking aspects of these results is the impact of Canadian turnover rates on opportunities for women. While the best-case scenario suggests that in Canada women could make up almost 47 percent of the members of the House of Commons within five elections, the same assumptions would yield less than 30 percent of the members of the American House.

The model illustrates very clearly the impact of low turnover rates in the United States. The results of these projections reinforce the conclusion that low legislative turnover rates can be a constraint to the election of women. Comparison of Canadian and American turnover rates suggests that in Canada, unlike the United States, this constraint is of limited importance.

Many observers of the Canadian House of Commons bemoan the high turnover rate in the membership of the House. C.E.S. Franks, for example, argues that the greatest single change that would strengthen Parliament would be to make MPs serve in the House longer (1987, 78). Franks and others argue that the significant number of inexperienced

Table 3.5
Canadian case–Women as percentage of elected MPs

Election	Scenario 1	Scenario 2	Scenario 3	Scenario 4	Scenario 5	Scenario 6
Initial	13.2	13.2	13.2	13.2	13.2	13.2
1	13.3	16.4	14.9	17.9	19.4	22.1
2	13.4	18.1	17.3	22.0	24.4	29.3
3	13.4	19.0	20.1	25.7	28.5	35.6
4	13.5	19.5	23.2	29.2	32.1	41.3
5	13.5	19.8	26.3	32.5	35.6	46.8

Table 3.6
American case–Women as percentage of elected representatives

Election	Scenario 1	Scenario 2	Scenario 3	Scenario 4	Scenario 5	Scenario 6
Initial	13.2	13.2	13.2	13.2	13.2	13.2
1	13.0	13.9	13.9	14.4	14.9	15.7
2	12.8	14.6	14.2	15.9	16.8	18.6
3	12.7	15.1	15.3	17.7	18.9	21.9
4	12.6	15.6	16.7	19.6	21.2	25.4
5	12.5	15.9	18.3	21.8	23.6	29.2

Note: Based on Canadian assumptions, current situation, but with American return rates.

members in any given Parliament weakens the effectiveness of the institution. The evidence presented in this study, however, suggests that the relatively high turnover rate increases the opportunities for women to enter the House, and therefore increases the societal responsiveness of the institution. It is apparent that the Canadian case strikes a reasonable balance between experience (fostered by stable membership) and accessibility and societal responsiveness (fostered by a rapid turnover rate, which allows entry to emerging social and political identities).

The model's projections also give some insight into other components of the opportunity structure facing women. First, these projections demonstrate that although removing bias against women will help somewhat, the proportion of female candidates must also increase. Scenario 2, which eliminates bias against women but does not increase the percentage of new candidates who are women, yields a House of

Figure 3.2
Women as percentage of all Canadian MPs — Various scenarios

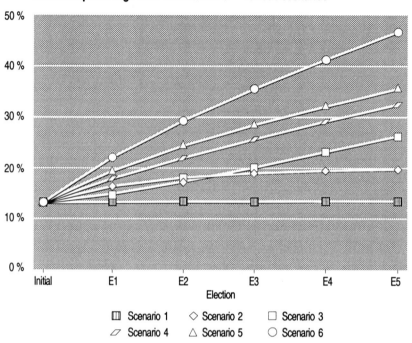

▥ Scenario 1	◇ Scenario 2	☐ Scenario 3
◪ Scenario 4	△ Scenario 5	○ Scenario 6

Commons whose membership is still less than 20 percent female after five elections. Scenario 3, which assumes a bias against women and a 3 percent increase each election in the proportion of new candidates who are women, yields a more rapid increase in the proportion of women in the House. Removing bias against women and gradually increasing the proportion of new candidates who are women (scenario 4) yields a 30 percent female membership in the House by the fifth election.

Second, these projections demonstrate that bias toward female candidates, which is to say affirmative action, will hasten the election of significant numbers of women. Scenario 6, which projects a House that is 47 percent female by the fifth election, assumes a 6 percent bias in favour of women. This means that women would have to be given advantages (primarily in the form of "safe" ridings) in the measure that they are now denied them. This entails an unprecedented commitment to affirmative action by the political parties at both the national and the local level.[6] The highly decentralized nature of the nomination process makes it extremely difficult for parties to implement such an affirmative action program effectively.

Therefore, rather than looking at voluntary vacancy and incumbency rates as barriers to the election of women, it may be useful to look at the relatively high legislative turnover rate in the House of Commons as providing an opportunity for women that does not exist in the United States and other comparable countries with low turnover rates.

Although it is evident that vacancy and incumbency rates are parameters that partially define the opportunity structure for women candidates, it should not be concluded that these factors significantly deter the election of women. There is no lack of open ridings or vulnerable incumbents in a typical Canadian general election. If all parties had nominated women in half of the constituencies that they had identified as winnable in the two most recent elections, the proportion of women in the House of Commons would be much greater than the current 13.2 percent.

CONCLUSION

This examination of the relationship between legislative turnover and the election of women to the Canadian House of Commons suggests that the turnover rate in the House creates an opportunity for women rather than a barrier. Elections characterized by high turnover (usually accompanied by a change in government) have, in recent years, led to substantial increases in the number of women elected. This suggests that the constraints facing women lie elsewhere, most notably in the recruitment and nomination phases of the electoral process, as well as in the supply of women willing to run.

This conclusion has implications for both Canadian and American observers. Those observers who, like Darcy, Welsh and Clark, blame the persistent under-representation of women in the United States on incumbency should examine the Canadian case. Even with its relatively high turnover rate, the membership of the House of Commons is far from representative in terms of gender. While a lower turnover rate would exacerbate the situation, other factors are clearly responsible for the under-representation of women. This suggests that the dearth of women in elected office is not a situation that will, all other things being equal, disappear over time. Rather, systemic barriers exist: they are only masked by low legislative turnover rates.

Certain reforms to the Canadian electoral system, notably limits on the number of terms an MP can serve, could encourage a higher legislative turnover rate, thereby possibly increasing the rate at which women enter the House. Such measures, however, would seriously impair the functioning of the House of Commons by robbing the institution of members with experience and expertise (see Franks 1987). In fact, it is apparent that the turnover rate in the House of Commons approximates an optimal balance between the competing objectives of rapid turnover to create opportunity for the election of women and slow turnover to foster experienced members of Parliament. Thus, term limitations and other reforms designed to increase the turnover rate are both unnecessary and probably harmful in the Canadian case.

The model used in this study also demonstrates that the number of women in the House of Commons can increase rapidly if the number of nonincumbent female candidates increases and women are no longer placed disproportionately in unwinnable ridings. The political parties, as the primary agents of recruitment and as the gatekeepers of the political process, must change their recruitment and nomination practices if there is to be substantial change in the number of women in the House of Commons. Although this is by no means an easy task, Canadian parties do enjoy an advantage in the form of the high turnover rate that characterizes the Canadian electoral system.

NOTES

The author gratefully acknowledges helpful comments from Kathy Megyery and two anonymous reviewers.

1. For a discussion of these and other factors affecting the election of women in Canada, see Brodie (1985), as well as other studies in this volume.

2. Incumbency is calculated as the number of incumbent MPs who are re-elected as a percentage of all incumbent members who stood for re-election. In 1980, the incumbency rate for women was 92%; the rate for all incumbents was 85%. In 1984, the rate for women was 68%, and the rate for all candidates was 69%. In 1988, the rates for women and for all candidates were 71% and 75%, respectively.

3. In 1984, 13% of all successful challengers (candidates who defeated an incumbent MP) were women, while only 10% of all candidates elected were women. In 1988, 19% of all successful challengers were women, while only 13% of all candidates elected were women.

4. The American electoral system is, in fact, unique in this regard. In other Western democracies with both single-member plurality and proportional representation systems, the central importance of party discipline makes the individual attributes of the candidate much less important than that candidate's party allegiance.

5. Probabilities in the model are calculated as follows:

Man re-elected	$p_1 = m_i \cdot r_m$
Woman elected	$p_2 = m_i \cdot (1 - r_m) \cdot (w + b)$
Man elected	$p_3 = m_i \cdot (1 - r_m) \cdot [(1 - w) - b]$
Woman re-elected	$p_4 = f_i \cdot r_f$
Woman elected	$p_5 = f_i \cdot (1 - r_f) \cdot (w + b)$
Man elected	$p_6 = f_i \cdot (1 - r_f) \cdot [(1 - w) - b]$

Men as proportion
of legislature = $p_1 + p_3 + p_6$

Women as proportion
of legislature = $p_2 + p_4 + p_5$

where m = men as proportion of old legislature
  f_i = women as proportion of old legislature
    (these variables are based on the result from the
    previous election in the model)
  r_m = return rate for male incumbents
  r_f = return rate for female incumbents
    (these parameters are based on the average of the
    return rates for men and women in the 1984 and
    1988 elections)
  b = bias for or against new female candidates
    (measured as difference between women as a percentage
    of candidates and women as a percentage of MPs)
  w = women as proportion of new candidates
    (these parameters are set to reflect different possible
    scenarios)

6. A noteworthy exception to this is the Ontario NDP, who in 1989 adopted affirmative action guidelines for nomination and candidacy. These guidelines specify that winnable or "priority" ridings should be identified and that 60 percent of the candidates in these seats should be women.

REFERENCES

Andersen, Kristi, and Stuart Thorson. 1984. "Congressional Turnover and the Election of Women." *Western Political Quarterly* 37 (March): 143–56.

Bashevkin, Sylvia. 1985. *Toeing the Lines: Women and Party Politics in English Canada*. Toronto: University of Toronto Press.

Barrie, Doreen, and Roger Gibbins. 1989. "Parliamentary Careers in the Canadian Federal State." *Canadian Journal of Political Science* 22:137–45.

Brodie, Janine. 1985. *Women and Politics in Canada*. Toronto: McGraw-Hill Ryerson.

Burrell, Barbara. 1988. "The Political Opportunity of Women Candidates for the U.S. House of Representatives in 1984." *Women and Politics* 8 (1): 51–67.

Cain, Bruce, John Ferejohn and Morris Fiorina. 1987. *The Personal Vote: Constituency Service and Electoral Independence.* Cambridge: Harvard University Press.

Carroll, Susan J. 1985. *Women as Candidates in American Politics.* Bloomington: Indiana University Press.

Clarke, Harold D., Jane Jenson, Lawrence LeDuc and Jon H. Pammett. 1991. *Absent Mandate: Interpreting Change in Canadian Elections.* 2d ed. Toronto: Gage Publications.

Courtney, John. 1985. "The Size of Canada's Parliament: An Assessment of the Implications of a Larger House of Commons." In *Institutional Reforms for Representative Government.* Vol. 38 of the research studies of the Royal Commission on the Economic Union and Development Prospects for Canada. Toronto: University of Toronto Press.

Darcy, R., and James Choike. 1986. "A Formal Analysis of Legislative Turnover: Women Candidates and Legislative Representation." *American Journal of Political Science* 30:237–55.

Darcy, R., Susan Welch and Janet Clark. 1987. *Women, Elections and Representation.* New York: Longman.

Docherty, David. 1990a. "Are Politicians Rational Actors? Political Careers in the Canadian House of Commons." M.A. thesis, McMaster University.

———. 1990b. "The Size of the House of Commons: Implications for Reform." Paper prepared for the Royal Commission on Electoral Reform and Party Financing. Ottawa.

Ferejohn, John, and Brian Gaines. 1991. "The Personal Vote in Canada." In *Representation, Integration and Political Parties in Canada*, ed. Herman Bakvis. Vol. 14 of the research studies of the Royal Commission on Electoral Reform and Party Financing. Ottawa and Toronto: RCERPF/Dundurn.

Franks, C.E.S. 1987. *The Parliament of Canada.* Toronto: University of Toronto Press.

Frizzell, Alan, Jon Pammett and Anthony Westell. 1989. *The Canadian General Election of 1988.* Ottawa: Carleton University Press.

Inter-Parliamentary Union. 1988. *Participation of Women in Political Life and in the Decision Making Process: A World Survey as of 1 April 1988.* Geneva: International Centre for Parliamentary Documentation.

Krashinsky, Michael, and William J. Milne. 1985. "Additional Evidence on the Effect of Incumbency in Canadian Elections." *Canadian Journal of Political Science* 18:155–65.

Nechemias, Carol. 1987. "Changes in the Election of Women to U.S. State Legislative Seats." *Legislative Studies Quarterly* 12 (February): 125–42.

Penniman, Howard R., ed. 1988. *Canada at the Polls, 1984*. Durham: Duke University Press for the American Enterprise Institute for Public Policy Research.

Randall, Vicky. 1982. *Women and Politics*. London: Macmillan.

Rydon, Joan. 1986. *A Federal Legislature: The Australian Commonwealth Parliament 1901–1980*. Melbourne: Oxford University Press.

Vallance, Elizabeth. 1979. *Women in the House: A Study of Women Members of Parliament*. London: Athlone Press.

Vallance, Elizabeth, and Elizabeth Davies. 1986. *Women of Europe: Women MEPs and Equality Policy*. Cambridge: Cambridge University Press.

Welch, Susan. 1978. "Recruitment of Women to Public Office: A Discriminant Analysis." *Western Political Quarterly* 31 (September): 372–80.

Williams, Christine B. 1990. "Women, Law and Politics: Recruitment Patterns in the Fifty States." *Women and Politics* 10 (3):103–23.

4

WOMEN AND CANDIDACIES FOR THE HOUSE OF COMMONS

Lynda Erickson

As a pivotal stage in the process through which the composition of our political élite is determined, candidate selection has attracted critical attention from those concerned with the gender imbalance in Canada's Parliament.[1] In particular, the parties' weak record in nominating women has been targeted by various women as a crucial issue in the campaign for better representation in the political sphere (Canadian Advisory Council on the Status of Women (CACSW) 1988; Brodie and Vickers 1981; Brodie 1985). The large national parties have responded to pressures from the women's community with a variety of programs, yet, notwithstanding apparent party interest, progress for women in the selection process has been slow. Compared with men, the number of women contesting local constituency seats remains few, and their proportions decline even more where their party is likely to win the riding. As a result, in the last election only 13 percent of the elected members of the House of Commons were women.

The objectives of this study are twofold. The first is to examine party selection procedures to see whether particular features of it work against or in favour of more women being nominated, especially in ridings where they have a chance of winning. The second is to consider various proposals for increasing the number of women in competitive party candidacies. Two sets of data are used for analysis of the selection process. The first set consists of data on party candidates and constituency election results compiled from official election statistics.[2] The other comes from the results of a survey conducted among local party associations following the 1988 general election.[3] The survey, designed specifically to study the nomination process, was sent to the official agents for all candidates of the three major parties represented in the House of Commons. The returns, which were well distributed across parties and across regions of the country, provide a good cross-section of the local associations that selected candidates for this election.

This study is divided into four sections. The first looks at the national party organizations and their activities with respect to women candidates, including their historical record in selecting women and their current programs relevant to women and the nomination process. The second section reviews the pattern of female candidacies in the 1988 election using official election statistics. The third examines the survey data in order to characterize the circumstances of local nominations and to identify the factors that encourage or discourage the selection of women. The final section discusses proposals for increasing the number of women candidates.

THE PARTIES AND WOMEN CANDIDATES

The Historical Record

Until the 1984 election, the historical record of women and party candidacies was a particularly meagre one. In the 1960s, when the women's movement began to direct public attention to the absence of women in positions of political power, fewer than 4 percent of all the candidates for the House of Commons were women. Though the numbers of women contesting seats increased in the 1970s, much of this increase occurred among so-called fringe candidates. By 1980 more than two-thirds of the women nominated were running for one of the minor parties or as independents (Brodie 1985, 21); among the major parties, only 8 percent of the candidates were women.

In comparison with earlier elections, the changes that occurred in 1984 were substantial. A majority of the women who stood for Parliament that year did so under the label of one of the major parties, and those parties almost doubled their number of women candidates. Eight percent of the Progressive Conservative candidates were women, while for the Liberals it was 15 percent and in the New Democratic Party (NDP) 23 percent. As a result, the representation of women in the House of Commons virtually doubled to almost 10 percent. But while important, such changes did not mark a transformation in the role of women in national elections. A disproportionate number nominated by the major parties were still placed in traditionally unwinnable constituencies, and the percentage who won their seats remained smaller than the percentage of male candidates who won.[4]

The increases that had been achieved were in apparent response to changes in the broader political environment. First, the women's movement in Canada had grown in visibility and organizational strength during the debate over the *Canadian Charter of Rights and Freedoms* in the early 1980s.[5] As a result, its calls for more women in Parliament seemed to be taken seriously by the various political parties. Second, the parties themselves were increasingly convinced of the relevance of a gender strategy to their overall popularity. As opinion polls began to suggest that the parties could suffer, among women voters, from a public image of insensitivity to the concerns of women, having women standard-bearers came to be seen as one element of an appropriate gender strategy (Brodie 1985).

One response by the parties to the call for greater numbers of women was financial. Shortly before the 1984 election, the New Democrats and the Liberals established special funds to assist their parties' women candidates in their election bids. The Conservatives established a similar fund shortly after the election (Kome 1985; CACSW 1988).

There were other responses as well.[6] In various public speeches and party pronouncements, the leaders attempted to demonstrate their interest in expanding the number of women candidates their parties nominated. And party workshops for women, including some on becoming a candidate, were held in various parts of the country. These activities specifically targeted to women were, however, more extensive and systematic in the NDP. The national NDP was more likely to be involved in the organization and sponsorship of such programs, while among the Liberals and Conservatives, programs such as the workshops for women were usually initiated locally. The NDP's activities on the candidate issue were part of a larger program directed toward achieving gender equality within the party. In 1983, for example, that party had passed a constitutional resolution that required gender parity in the composition of the national executive.

But in their efforts to increase the number of women candidates, all three parties faced the reality of a highly localized system of candidate selection. This made it difficult for the national organizations to involve themselves more directly in local nominations. As one party official observed about the role of national parties in the selection of women, "it is very much still on the encouragement level."

Party Activities and the 1988 Election

In the period before the 1988 election, the leaders of the national parties again made it clear they would like more women to run as candidates of their party. But the parties still lacked the mechanisms to institute such goals. A member of the National Women's Liberal Commission raised this issue of the inadequacy of party mechanisms at a national Liberal party meeting in 1986. Yet although she found support among many of the women attending, there was no official response to the problem.

The NDP had a national party committee that attempted to identify ridings where women might be considering running, and it targeted such women for encouragement.[7] Further, in what it considered to be a policy that would encourage new types of candidates, like women, to run for the party, the national organization put a freeze on nominations from March 1987 until January of the following year. The national party office also continued its earlier practice of organizing regional workshops for women, including ones on candidacies in the party, and in the spring of 1987, it held a conference in Ottawa for women who were running for nominations or were potential contestants for nominations. But, with the 1988 election promising to bring a better result for the NDP, women contemplating candidacies may have found that the local line-ups for nomination were more formidable than in the 1984 election.[8]

For the Liberals, the process of identifying and encouraging women candidates seems to have been more decentralized and informal. The national party itself did not organize programs to train women; where such activities took place they tended to be undertaken on a local basis by individuals within the Women's Commission. The National Women's Liberal Commission published brochures on how to contest a local candidacy, but they were sent to riding organizations and not targeted to individual women.

For the Conservatives, bringing more women into the system posed a problem of somewhat different dimensions than it did for the Liberals or the New Democrats because the party had a very large number of sitting members who intended to seek reselection. Among the constituency associations that responded to the nomination survey, 62 percent of the Conservative ones had a sitting member seeking reselection compared with 7 percent of the Liberal and 12 percent of the NDP associations. Since all three parties tend to protect incumbents from challenge within their local associations, efforts to increase the number of women candidates would be limited to that minority of seats with either no incumbent or one not seeking reselection. As with the Liberals, Conservative activities, such as workshops directed specifically to women, tended to be localized and not orchestrated by the national party. In late May 1988, there was a national conference for Conservative women sponsored by the National Progressive Conservative Women's

Federation and the party's Women's Bureau, but its focus was primarily the overall involvement of women in the party and in election campaigns, and little attention was given to the question of how to become a candidate.[9]

Among the minor parties, activities concerning candidates were primarily directed to finding standard-bearers, a task which left little time and few resources for programs specifically directed to women.

WOMEN CANDIDATES AND THE 1988 ELECTION

In the 1988 election, 19 percent of all candidates who filed nomination papers were women, but their distribution among parties and provinces was uneven. In the provinces, with the exception of Prince Edward Island, the proportion of women candidates was highest in the largest and highly urban provinces of Quebec and Ontario (see table 4.1). Perhaps surprisingly, given they were the pioneers of female suffrage in Canada, the Prairie provinces were below the norm for women candidacies. In Manitoba, where women first achieved the right to vote, only 9 percent of those nominated were female. It was in Atlantic Canada, however, that both the highest and lowest provincial percentages were recorded. In Prince Edward Island, fully 36 percent of the 14 candidates nominated for seats were women, while New Brunswick had the lowest record of women candidates with a mere 7 percent. But the

Table 4.1
Women candidates in the 1988 general election by province

	%	N
Atlantic		
Newfoundland (23)	13	3
Nova Scotia (46)	15	7
New Brunswick (43)	7	3
Prince Edward Island (14)	36	5
Quebec (386)	22	86
Ontario (513)	21	107
Prairies		
Manitoba (86)	9	8
Saskatchewan (57)	12	7
Alberta (167)	19	31
British Columbia (226)	19	43

Source: Office of the Chief Electoral Officer of Canada.

Note: Figures in parentheses represent total numbers of candidates.

Table 4.2
Women candidates in the major parties

Party	%	N
Progressive Conservative	13	37
Liberal	18	53
NDP	28	84

Source: Office of the Chief Electoral Officer of Canada.

Prince Edward Island figures must be placed in context. Three of the four women candidates in the province ran for the NDP, and in the context of that province's federal politics, the NDP might well be considered a fringe party: it received just 7 percent of the province's votes in the 1984 and 1988 general elections.

In party terms, the patterns established in 1984 were repeated in 1988 (table 4.2). The three major parties again ran a majority (59 percent) of the women candidates in the election,[10] the distribution of these candidates among the three parties remained uneven, and the NDP still nominated the most women while the Conservatives nominated the fewest. Only 13 percent of Conservative party candidates were women, compared to 28 percent of the NDP who were female. Eighteen percent of the candidates nominated by the Liberals were women.

The uneven distribution of women candidates among parties was also apparent in the minor parties. The regional and religious parties had the lowest proportion of women running:[11] the Confederation of Regions party, the Christian Heritage party, and the Reform Party had, respectively, 8, 10 and 11 percent women candidates. On the other hand, only the Green party and the Communist party ran more women than the norm: 22 and 38 percent, respectively.[12]

The pattern within both the major and minor parties suggests that party ideology may be a factor in the selection of women.[13] Among the minor parties, the regional parties and the Christian Heritage party tend to be associated with right-wing policies on social and economic issues, whereas the policies of the Green party and, of course, the Communist party are left-wing. Among the major parties, the left-wing/right-wing distinction is more problematic, especially between the Liberals and Conservatives. However, if we accept recent characterizations of the Conservatives as a centre-right party, with the Liberals more centrist and the New Democrats on the left,[14] again we find female candidates are more likely to be nominated by parties of the left and least likely to be nominated by parties of the right. How, or if, ideology works to effect this result among the major parties will be explored below with the assistance of the survey data. For the minor parties, we simply note the pattern.

Women and Good Seats

Whatever the party distribution of women candidates, more important for concerns about gender parity in the legislature is whether women are nominated in ridings that are winnable for their party. Do parties choose to nominate women primarily in losing ridings, or are winnable seats distributed proportionately?

Finding an answer to this question seems, on the face of it, straightforward – simply use each local association's comparative performance in the last election as a measure of competitiveness. However, it is necessary to take into account the changes in constituency boundaries that occurred with the redistribution of 1987, and, given the atypical nature of the 1984 election, adjustments should be made for the unusually high Conservative vote. Yet, even taking such factors into account, using only one indicator based on the 1984 results may be insufficient as an indicator of local competitiveness at the time candidates were selected because of the fluidity of the public's party preferences, as demonstrated in the opinion polls in the two years prior to the 1988 election (Frizzell 1989). Moreover, if we are interested in the effect of competitiveness on party activity, perceptions of local competitiveness would seem to be a critical element in this effect. Accordingly, two measures of competitiveness were developed: one was based on local party performance in the previous (1984) general election, the other one was taken from a question in the nomination survey about party views of their competitiveness in the riding.[15] Because the former measure is based on aggregate data, we can use it to look at the candidates from virtually all the local associations of the three major parties in the country.[16] With the latter measure, we are limited to examining the local associations represented in the survey.

For the performance-based measure, a party's percentage lead or lag behind the winner in the 1984 election was calculated.[17] Four categories were then developed, taking into account the atypically high Conservative vote.[18] The survey measure also had four response categories available to the respondents; they were asked whether their party considered the local seat to be "safe," "good chance," "unlikely"or "hopeless." Because only the three largest parties elected members in 1988 or were considered competitive enough to do so, the analysis below will be limited to those parties.

Results at both the aggregate level, using the performance measure, and in the survey data, using the perception variable, suggest that
women are still not being nominated in safe seats to the same degree
as are men. According to the aggregate data in table 4.3, only 12 percent of the women nominated by the three parties were nominated to
candidacies characterized as safe, an advantage enjoyed by 25 percent of the male candidates. Women were also less likely than men to
be nominated to good-chance candidacies and more likely to be
nominated for hopeless candidacies. From the perspective of local associations and their judgement of their own competitiveness, women
were also underrepresented in safe candidacies, although they were
not as badly placed in the other competitive categories. Indeed, a slightly

Table 4.3
Women and nominations in competitive seats

	Aggregate figures (Performance-based measure)	
	Sex of candidate	
Competitiveness of local party	Female (%)	Male (%)
Safe seat	12	25
Good chance	18	26
Unlikely	14	12
Hopeless	56	38
N	(171)	(706)
	Survey results (Perception-based measure)	
	Sex of candidate	
Competitiveness of local party	Female (%)	Male (%)
Safe seat	10	22
Good chance	52	47
Unlikely	32	24
Hopeless	6	7
N	(69)	(275)

Source: The aggregate figures were calculated from figures provided by the Office of the
Chief Electoral Officer of Canada.

larger proportion of the women (52 percent) than the men (47 percent) were nominated by local associations that considered their electoral prospects good. The discrepancy between the gender differences in the two sets of data is largely explained by the optimism of the opposition parties, especially the NDP, about their electoral prospects compared with their performance in the 1984 election. The local associations of these parties both nominated more women than did the Conservatives and were more likely to judge their electoral prospects as better than our performance variable categorized them to be.

THE SELECTION OF WOMEN AND THE LOCAL NOMINATION PROCESS

Incumbency

From what is known of reselection, it should be expected that incumbency accounts for some of the difference in the proportions of women and men candidates running in safe seats. Safe seats are much more likely to have incumbents seeking reselection, and the norms of all three parties work in favour of incumbents. Although normally subject to nomination meetings as are other candidates, incumbents are seldom challenged by other prospective nominees at these meetings. In the survey, only one in eight incumbents faced competition at their selection meeting, and four-fifths of the local associations that considered their seat to be safe had incumbents seeking renomination.[19] All of the incumbents in safe seats were reselected, but only 9 percent of them were women.

Clearly, incumbency presents the most significant short-term obstacle to women's candidacies in competitive ridings and hence to greater gender parity in the House of Commons. Although women who do become members of Parliament are as immune to challenges as their male counterparts – none of the women members in the constituencies represented in the survey were challenged at their reselection meetings – the protection that party norms give to their members of Parliament inevitably reduces the opportunities for women.

There are, however, some factors that moderate the effects of incumbency. While it does restrict the pace of change, incumbency is less limiting in Canada than in many political systems similar to ours. The higher turnover rate in the House, partly a result of the lower proportion of safe seats in Canada, provides some explanation for the higher percentage of women sitting in our national legislature compared with countries like Britain and the United States (Blake 1991). There is also some hint in the survey data that norms concerning incumbents may be less protective than they once were. In our sample, 12 percent of the

Table 4.4
Women aspirants and the competitiveness of nominations
(percentages)

	Woman sought nomination	Only men sought nomination
Acclamation	39	71
Competition	61	29
N	(106)	(211)

incumbents were challenged at their nomination meetings, and three of them were not reselected.[20] This moderation in party norms may subsequently be of some benefit to women, but the survey suggests women (like men) are more reluctant to enter politics by challenging incumbents than by seeking candidacies in constituency associations without a sitting member.[21] Moreover, in spite of the number of challenged incumbents in the 1988 election, it is unlikely that the protection given incumbents will alter much more in the near future.

Not only does incumbency tend to protect safe seats from challenge by women, it also means that when women do seek nominations they are more likely to face competition because nominations without incumbents are more contested. In the survey, 61 percent of those local associations where a woman sought to be the candidate had more than one nominee for that position (table 4.4). By contrast, in those associations where no woman ran for nomination there was competition in only 29 percent of the cases. As a result, almost half (47 percent) of the women candidates running for one of the three major parties had faced competitive selection compared with less than a third (31 percent) of the men candidates.

Competition

While incumbency exacerbates the competition women face when they seek party nominations, it alone does not explain the more competitive circumstances women face when they seek nominations. Table 4.5 shows that, even in associations with no incumbent contesting the candidacy, women were more likely to have to win a contested nomination. This finding holds both for associations that see themselves as electorally competitive and for those that do not (table 4.6). The route to electoral office is, for women more than men, a two-stage struggle: one at the nomination stage, the other at election time. This is not to suggest that competitive selection should be viewed negatively: the implications of competitive

Table 4.5
Women aspirants and the competitiveness of nominations: non-incumbent associations
(percentages)

	Woman sought nomination	Only men sought nomination
Acclamation	34	65
Competition	65	35
N	(92)	(155)

Table 4.6
Women aspirants and the competitiveness of nominations by electoral competitiveness of local association

	Woman sought nomination		Only men sought nomination	
	%	N	%	N
Safe or good chance candidacies				
Acclamation	30	15	49	42
Competition	70	35	51	35
Unlikely or hopeless candidacies				
Acclamation	44	15	84	56
Competition	56	19	15	10

Notes: Non-incumbent associations only.

selection for the parties, and for internal party democracy, appear to be primarily positive. The current selection process gives local members a point of input and influence within the party structure, but without choice among competitors for the post, this input – and indeed local party democracy – is likely to suffer. However, for individual candidates, the implications of competition at the selection stage are also financial. According to the survey, those candidates who had faced competition at their selection meetings spent significantly more on their nomination campaigns than did those who were chosen by acclamation.[22] This means that women, whose personal financial resources are typically less than those of men in similar circumstances, are often in the position of having to spend more money to enter federal politics because they face a competitive nomination process.[23] Thus, while the three parties have special funds to assist their women candidates in the election campaign that follows nomination, this is of no assistance at the stage in electoral politics that appears to be more crucial for the representation of women: the pre-nomination period.

Although perhaps running under a financial disadvantage, women did do as well as men in nomination battles. In the survey, of those associations in which both women and men competed for nomination, a woman was selected 54 percent of the time. Like the larger electorate, local activists who participate in selection ballots show little evidence of resistance to women politicians.[24] If decentralized nomination is a factor that works against the selection of women, its effects begin before the stage at which local members choose among potential candidates. The problem seems to be that fewer women than men place their names on selection ballots, and as a result, a majority of associations do not have any women contesting nominations.[25]

Increasing Supply

The lack of women contesting nominations suggests that in the debate over whether the problem of women's representation is an issue of supply – not enough women are willing to run for politics – or one of demand – there are barriers to women's participation in the parties – the answer is one of supply. But the data on party activities suggest the issue is more complex: the number of women who do seek selection can be modified by party practices. Recruitment activities at both the local and national level can target and encourage women to seek nominations, especially in associations where no incumbent is seeking reselection.

At the local level, search committees can be used both to encourage competitive selection and to encourage women to run. Table 4.7 demonstrates that such structures can be especially effective for women. Among associations without an incumbent MP standing for reselection, those

Table 4.7
Local party search committees and women aspirants/candidates

	Local association had candidate search committee			
	Yes		No	
	%	N	%	N
Women sought nomination	43	64	27	26
Woman candidate selected	30	46	16	17

Note: Non-incumbent associations only.

with search committees were more likely to have had at least one woman seeking the local nomination and to have selected a woman as their candidate.

The view that local recruitment practices can be encouraging for women is further supported by responses to another question in the survey. Respondents were asked whether their local association had to talk its candidate into running. Among those few that did, 29 percent had female candidates. Among those that did not, 19 percent had candidates who were women.[26]

The figures on local recruitment activities also suggest one of the means by which party differences in women candidacies have arisen. Again, looking at only those associations in which no incumbent stood for reselection, the figures in tables 4.8 and 4.9 show that the NDP was more likely to have local search committees,[27] to produce female aspirants to run for nomination when such committees did exist and to nominate women in those constituencies. For the Liberals, the differences produced by search committees are not statistically significant, but the direction of the numbers is consistent with the pattern among the New Democrats. For the Conservatives, however, the figures are anomalous. Although based on a very small number of constituencies, the findings on the Conservatives suggest that while search committees can be a factor, they do not guarantee the selection of more women.

Influence from other levels of the party organizations was also a factor in the nomination of more women. As we described above, the national leadership of all three parties had indicated their interest in increasing the number of women candidates, but this interest was pursued most systematically in the NDP. Our survey data reflect this. When asked if there was encouragement from their national party to choose a woman candidate, 15 percent of the respondents said there was, and

Table 4.8
Search committees by party

Party	Local search committee		
	Yes (%)	No (%)	N
NDP	70	30	113
Liberal	54	46	110
Conservative	51	49	43

Note: Non-incumbent associations only.

Table 4.9
Party search committees and female aspirants and candidates

Party	Search committee		
	Yes (%)	No (%)	N
NDP			
Woman aspirant(s)	52	28	107
Woman candidate	42	18	112
Liberal			
Woman aspirant(s)	37	24	99
Woman candidate	20	14	105
Conservative			
Woman aspirant(s)	26	30	39
Woman candidate	10	19	42

Notes: Non-incumbent associations only. Cell entries are percentages of local associations in which at least one woman ran for the nomination.

four-fifths of that 15 percent were NDP associations. Excluding those associations with incumbents prepared to run again, only 2 and 7 percent, respectively, of Conservative and Liberal associations indicated there was such encouragement, compared with 40 percent of NDP riding organizations.

Although indirect and limited in its reach, national encouragement did seem to be effective when practised. It resulted in more women competing for candidacies and in more women candidates being chosen, at least among associations with no incumbent seeking reselection. In our survey, of those associations that indicated they were encouraged by their national party to choose a woman, 59 percent had at least one woman seeking to run for them, and 53 percent nominated a woman candidate. By comparison, in associations reporting no such encouragement, 29 percent had a woman seek nomination, and only 17 percent chose a woman candidate (table 4.10).[28]

Summary

Survey evidence points to a number of features of the nomination process that seem to work against the participation of women as candidates in the election process, especially in ridings in which their party is well placed competitively. Party norms about incumbency are important, and the financial strain of competitive selection is also hinted at in our data, albeit indirectly. The greater resources available to prospective male candidates, whether from personal finances or contacts with

Table 4.10
Women aspirants and national party encouragement

	Local association encouraged to select a woman candidate			
	Yes		No	
	%	N	%	N
Woman sought nomination				
Yes	59	26	29	51
No	41	18	71	123
Woman candidate selected				
Yes	53	25	17	31
No	47	22	83	156

Note: Non-incumbent associations only.

others who are able to contribute financially to a selection battle, may mean some women simply do not enter the contest.

On the other hand, local search committees can contribute to the number of women willing to seek candidacies, as can national party efforts to influence nominations through encouragement. But the data suggest that neither local committees nor pronouncements by national party leaders are sufficient to produce women nominees at the local level. Search committees must have an agenda that focuses on encouraging women, and regional and national party programs for women need to be systematic to produce substantial change in the nomination numbers.

WHAT CAN BE DONE TO INCREASE THE NUMBER OF WOMEN?

Proposals for Party Action

Although incumbency is a factor inhibiting change in the number of women in the House of Commons, it is unrealistic to expect substantial modification in local practices concerning sitting members. Moreover, it is not clear what kinds of party provisions in this area would clearly benefit women, yet not weaken our legislature. In a system in which the turnover of members of Parliament is so high that political experience among legislators is an issue of concern (Franks 1987), it is important to avoid changes that would seriously undermine the political arena as a career alternative.[29] If incumbents not only face the insecurity of re-election, but also are routinely deselected, a political career in national politics will become even less attractive than it now is.

If we can expect, at most, modest change in the area of incumbents, are there other activities that national party organizations can undertake that have clear potential to increase the representation of women in this arena? The answer indicated by the survey and interview data is yes. A comparison of the success of the New Democratic Party with that of the other two parties in the study suggests that systematic efforts by a national party committee to identify and then encourage prospective women candidates across the country can have an effect. Indeed, parties should be encouraged to do this for virtually all minimally competitive (non-incumbent) constituencies. Even on a more modest level, efforts by national organizations to identify women across the country who might consider contesting a candidacy could be expanded into a more formalized system. For example, a provision adopted at the national Liberal party convention in June 1990, to strike a task force to compile a "talent bank" of women for nomination to leading party positions, could be modified so that local associations would be encouraged to use the talent bank in their search for prospective candidates. On the program level, nationally directed workshops that target women and specifically address the question of candidacy do seem to encourage women to come forward. However, although nationally sponsored, such programs are likely to be more effective, given the limited resources available to many women, if delivered at the regional and local level. Further, the timing of such programs is crucial: they are more likely to have some effect if they are held at least a year in advance of a likely election call and before the final line-up of prospective candidates forms.

In other policy areas, the practice of prohibiting selection meetings until late in a Parliament's tenure could be adopted by all parties. This may be of particular benefit to women because their work and family lives make it difficult for them to give a commitment to a candidacy very far in advance of an election. On finances, centralized party funds for selection battles could reduce the personal cost of campaigns. Whether such funds would simply encourage "fringe" contestants or make the selection of candidates effectively more competitive (and hence more democratic) will depend upon the conditions for nomination to selection ballots. Where such conditions are more stringent (at least in time requirements for membership), the latter result is more likely. For women, however, centralized funds, combined with some party limits on expenditures, will make candidacies financially more accessible.

Proposals for Wider Reform
Proposals for systematic modifications and reform have largely focused on four aspects of candidate selection that seem to limit its accessibility

to women: the privileged place of incumbents; the decentralized character of the nomination process; the financial burden of seeking selection; and the personal sacrifices required of national politicians.

The Privileged Place of Incumbents

Earlier, it was suggested that we can expect little change in party practices concerning incumbents and it was argued that provisions that would further undermine the career attraction of national politics should be avoided. Yet, incumbency remains one of the barriers to the increased representation of women. Putting legal limits on the length of legislative careers, an alternative suggested by women's groups in the United States as a way of addressing the problem of putting more women into their national legislature, may redress some of the gender imbalance in candidacies, but would add to the problem of career attractiveness.

A different means of addressing the incumbency issue would be to add new seats to the legislature. This would likely increase the number of women candidates running in competitive seats, but would it make a substantial change? In the aggregate data, women constituted only 13 percent of the candidates who ran in candidacies characterized as having a safe seat or a good chance of being elected. This percentage only increased to 17 when seats in which incumbents ran were excluded from the calculations. Thus, increasing the number of seats in the House would by itself not contribute to substantial change.

Decentralized Selection

Decentralized selection has been targeted as a problem for the selection of women for a variety of reasons. One of these, the notion that the grassroots membership prefers male candidates and, given the choice, opts for men to run for its party, is not borne out by our data. The problem with local selection seems to come from the curious summary effects of single-member versus list selection. It is simply more difficult to coordinate activities involving multiple decisions at the local level, even if these activities are primarily the encouragement of women. More intervention, such as singling out individual constituencies to redress the gender imbalance, may be viewed from the local perspective as limiting equality of opportunity. It is easier to balance central lists of candidates, and to do so seems to agree more readily with popular notions of equality.[30] As a result, some of the proposals for reform that have been voiced elsewhere involve changes to the electoral system itself, changes that would move parties in the direction of centralized-list systems for selection.

The most familiar and prevalent kinds of electoral arrangements using centralized lists of candidates are the various systems of proportional representation. Such systems differ in whether their lists are national, regional or local; whether the allocation of seats is national, regional or local; and whether and how voters can register choices for candidates within individual party lists. The implications for women of these different alternatives have seldom been investigated and, in the Canadian context, have attracted virtually no attention because the adoption of a system of proportional representation as our primary form of electing members to the House of Commons has not, to date, been seriously contemplated either by any government or by any major national party. The attachment Canadians have to a system in which one member of Parliament is elected from (and hence appears responsible to) one territorial constituency has apparently narrowed the practical alternatives for reform.

Public views of acceptable alternatives can also be said to have closed discussion on another alternative electoral system proposed by Christine Boyle (1983) in a study, "Home Rule for Women." Boyle argues that some form of separate representation of women should be included in our electoral system. There is, she suggests, no fundamental reason why geography should be the only basis for representation. Rather, given the different interests of women and men, gender should be a factor in drawing electoral boundaries. Women's and men's votes would be counted separately, and men and women would then elect separate members to our legislative arena. She argues that "men and women would, in effect, be sharing power" (ibid., 801). Such a system would undeniably increase the power of women, but among the public, the legitimacy of separate representation for women and men is questionable.

While proposals on this scale have not reached the political agenda, more modest suggestions for reform have. Although not initiated because of concerns for women's representation, these suggestions do have relevance here because they can be used to incorporate a partial-list system of selection. They were originally advanced in response to another perceived failure of our national parties: regional representation.[31] In the face of national parties that had distinct regional vacuums in their legislative representation, political scientists began to focus on the electoral system as a factor that at least exacerbated a problem of party, and hence governmental, representation. With a single-member plurality system, the regional representation in party caucuses has not accurately reflected parties' regional support in the popular vote. The solution, most reformers argued, was for some sort of system in which a number of new regional seats would be established. These seats would be used to top up the representation of parties to more closely reflect their percentage of the popular vote in each region. A party's regional representatives would come from lists prepared by its national or regional party structures. There would then be a dual system of representation: the current constituency representation would be combined with at-large regional members apportioned by the proportional calculations. For candidate selection, a list system of nomination for the regional seats would be added to the current system of local selection.

Such a system could benefit women. For those whose work and contacts within a party have been primarily local, the traditional route to candidacy would still be available. However, the regional lists would allow for a program of affirmative action by those parties committed to increasing their women legislators. If party lists were fixed, thus not allowing voters to rank their choices within a list, party candidates would not have to campaign publicly against their own party members in order to be elected, and women would not be faced with the kind of financial burden from selection that seems especially detrimental to them as a group.[32]

While the debate on electoral reform is beyond the focus of this study, it should be acknowledged that top-up proposals as outlined above are both comparatively modest and feasible. They preserve the virtues of the single-member system by retaining the local constituency representatives, while allowing some of the representational virtues of proportional representation. Although electoral reform is not a guarantee of more seats for women, it would increase the chances of improved gender representation.

Financial Reforms

It has already been suggested that the financial implications of seeking a party candidacy have particular consequences for women. Moreover, it is expected that the financial burden of seeking a competitive nomination will increase in the absence of party or governmental regulation. It is in this context of expected increases that proposals for maximum expenditure limits for pre-selection campaigns should be considered. While the prospect of further regulation of expenditures may create a burden for some candidates, the size of most local constituency associations and the requirements necessary for the communication of candidate information to members would suggest that large expenditures are not necessary for informed grassroots participation. With no large expenditures, reporting procedures need not be complicated. The problem with leaving such regulation to the parties themselves is illustrated in the experience of party leadership contests, where the exercise of setting expenditure limits typically becomes part of the leadership contest itself. There are few reasons to suppose government regulation would limit women's access to candidacies, and both our data and the comments by women party activists suggest there are reasons to think it would increase this accessibility.

Women and the National Political Arena

Earlier it was argued that one of the reasons for the underrepresentation of women in party candidacies is that fewer women than men put their names forward for selection. While it is apparent that party practices can go some way toward modifying the discrepancy in these numbers, reforms in other parts of our system are also called for. It seems the life of a national politician is not sufficiently attractive as a career option in this country (either for the short or long term). This appears to be especially true for women, but the evidence is also there for men. The survey of candidate selection indicated that, even excluding the local associations in which incumbents sought reselection, competition for local candidacies is the exception rather than the rule. In local organizations with no sitting member, 56 percent had uncontested nominations. Even in seats considered by the local party association to be safe for their party, 43 percent saw only one person seeking this safe candidacy.

For many women and men, the life of a member of Parliament may involve personal sacrifices that are simply too great. Few MPs in a country the size of Canada can live in their local constituencies when Parliament is sitting. This requires most members to keep two residences, and it means families must make choices that may involve considerable personal sacrifice on the part of spouses and children. Families must decide between moving to Ottawa or staying in their local constituency. Whatever the choice, family members usually find their spouse and/or parent must still spend considerable time away from them. Frequent travelling to local constituencies is a fact of life for most Canadian members of Parliament.

The high turnover of seats in the Canadian system means the disruptions of distance and travel are greatly compounded by the insecurity of tenure in the position. Not even the timing of the next election is fixed. The personal toll on families as well as the politicians themselves is considerable.[33] All of this is best known by those most active in political parties: in other words, just those we might expect to become competitors for local nominations. The impact of this knowledge may be especially great on women activists, given the modal pattern of family relationships, even in the 1990s.

Many of the circumstances of a politician's life are a function of the demands of a modern political system compounded by the territorial dimensions of the Canadian state, but there are aspects of our system which could be modified to ameliorate some of the conditions that discourage women (and men) from seeking national political office. One of these is the amount of time members are required to spend in Ottawa. A modified calendar for the House, one which would allow members to spend more time in their constituencies, could provide more flexibility to members and their families. The use of modern technology, like interactive video communication systems, could even allow members to register their votes in House divisions when they were out of Ottawa and in their local constituencies. Such changes should not mean virtual absence from Ottawa, but they could allow members to spend more time working in their local areas. Predictability for members' lives could be further improved by establishing a fixed term for Parliament, one that could only be altered by the defeat of a government. Such a provision could be instituted without constitutional change so long as the term remained within the constitutional requirements of a five-year limit to a Parliament.

It may well be suggested that these proposed changes are politically difficult, to say the least. The last change seems especially unlikely, given the advantage the choice of election timing gives to a government. Yet, the lack of competition for candidacies in our system and the opting out by women suggest we need to question seriously some of the conditions of national political life in Canada.

NOTES

1. There is little evidence either from public opinion polls or in aggregate analyses of voting patterns that voters pose a barrier to the election of women. Voters do not show particular preference for male politicians nor do they appear to vote disproportionately for male candidates when women and men run in similarly placed circumstances. This suggests the critical role the selection process plays in the representation of women in the House of Commons. Comparative analyses further reinforce this argument. What clearly distinguishes countries in which women are comparatively well represented in national legislatures is the number of women who are selected by parties to run as candidates for office (Norris 1987, chap. 6).

2. These data on election statistics and the women candidates who ran for the various parties came from the Office of the Chief Electoral Officer.

3. The survey was conducted jointly by the author and R. Kenneth Carty of the University of British Columbia. For further details on the response rate of the survey and the regional and partisan distribution of the returns see Carty and Erickson (1991).

4. Even in some of the constituencies where women did win, it was in ridings where their party had previously been uncompetitive. This was particularly true for many of the women who ran for the Conservatives in Quebec.

5. For the activities of the women's movement during the constitutional exercise see Hošek (1983).

6. The discussion on party activities in the 1984 and 1988 elections is based on interviews with officials or former officials from the three parties.

7. Sometimes the national party president or a party MP would phone these women to urge them to run.

8. In fact, according to the survey, fewer than one-third of NDP candidates actually faced competition at their selection meetings, and, as is shown below, when women did face competition for selection, they did well. But the prospects of competing against another well-placed competitor may have discouraged some women.

9. In a day devoted to political organization, there was one presentation of a woman's story about becoming a candidate.

10. By comparison, 56 percent of the male candidates ran for a major party.

11. This party analysis excludes the Parti Rhinocéros and Social Credit. The Rhinos do not consider themselves a serious party and are excluded for that reason. Social Credit is excluded because it ran only nine candidates.

12. In the remaining two parties, the Libertarian and Commonwealth, 15 and 19 percent, respectively, were women candidates.

13. The pattern observed here with respect to ideology is also documented in analyses of women's representation in European legislatures (Norris 1987).

14. For such a characterization of the differences between the Liberals and Conservatives based on analyses of the spending agendas of the parties see Graham (1990, chap.1). For a similar characterization of Conservative and Liberal party activists see Blake (1989).

15. The question put to the agents who received the questionnaire was, "When the party was nominating the candidate, how did the local association assess the chances of victory in the constituency?"

16. One Liberal association did not nominate a candidate in the 1988 election, and data are missing for three other associations. Results from four local associations are accordingly missing.

17. These percentages were calculated using the 1987 boundary changes. Vote transposition figures were publicly available by constituency from Elections Canada.

18. The Conservatives were assigned a 10 percent "handicap" for the top two categories of "safe" and "good chance" seats. Slightly larger adjustments

were made in the bottom two categories. For details on this measure see Carty and Erickson (1991). Clearly the cut-off points in this measure are somewhat arbitrary, and other analysts may place them differently. As a result, the author tested a number of different cut-off points but found the general story told by the figures was similar. Fewer women were candidates in "safe" or "good chance" ridings.

19. According to the aggregate data from election statistics, 25 percent of the major party candidates were incumbents.

20. Since there is no systematic evidence on challenges to incumbents from earlier years, any conclusions about changes in the protection afforded them must remain tentative. However, historical accounts suggest it was unusual for incumbents to face a local challenge (Williams 1981).

21. In only a quarter of the challenges to incumbents was a woman seeking to win the nomination over the sitting member: in other words, fewer than 3 percent of incumbents were challenged by a woman. As we illustrate below, substantially more of the non-incumbent constituencies had at least one woman contesting the nomination.

22. The average spending on the pre-selection campaign by those candidates who won their nominations by acclamation was reported to be $623. For those who faced competitive nomination meetings, this average was $2 685.

23. Prima facie evidence that women seeking to enter federal politics have fewer financial resources than their male counterparts comes from the survey data on pre-nomination spending. The women candidates in the survey who had faced competition at their selection meetings spent less than did men candidates who had faced competition. Yet, these women still spent more on their pre-nomination activities than did the men who did not face competition.

24. Local associations may in fact be more than even-handed when it comes to choosing between women and men candidates. In those associations that had at least one woman on their selection ballot, 46 percent had more men than women seeking selection, whereas only 10 percent had more women than men.

25. Even in constituencies with no local incumbent seeking reselection, only 37 percent had at least one woman seeking the nomination. By comparison, 85 percent of these constituencies had at least one man seeking the nomination.

26. The majority of these women candidates who were talked into running ran for local organizations whose electoral chances were judged to be at least "good." For the men candidates who were talked into running, a majority ran for organizations whose electoral chances were judged to be "unlikely" or "hopeless."

27. It was national party policy to encourage local associations to establish search committees.

28. Some of this effect may be partly the result of "selective hearing" of national party messages on the part of local associations. Those associations most disposed to choosing women candidates may have been more likely to interpret national party activities and communication as "encouragement to choose a woman candidate." How much of this effect is selective hearing independent of the activities of the national parties is impossible to estimate. However, the fact that most of the "encouragement" is reported by NDP constituencies, and interviews with various party officials and former officials suggested that the NDP activities in this regard were most centralized and systematic, does imply that party activities were relevant in producing these constituency assessments.

29. As Franks (1987) argues, political amateurism may contribute to the weakness of House members vis-à-vis the executive, the bureaucracy and private interest groups.

30. Party activists are, typically, protective of local control of nominations and usually reject proposals that would restrict local choice. Thus, surveys of party activists taken in the 1980s suggest members do not favour quota systems that they see as limiting their local choice (Carty and Erickson 1991). In 1991, however, the NDP national convention held in Halifax did pass motions establishing as a general policy that 50 percent of its riding associations should have women candidates and giving the party's Federal Council "the authority to set nomination rules to achieve affirmative action goals." The latter motion, a constitutional amendment, required a two-thirds majority to pass.

31. The literature on this issue is extensive. For a survey of some of the proposals to redress the problem see Irvine (1985).

32. On the benefits of fixed lists for parties see Irvine (1985).

33. In their information booklet for prospective candidates, the Reform Party comments on the stress of the job of an MP and the impact of the job on the lives of spouses and children.

REFERENCES

Blake, Donald E. 1989. "Division and Cohesion: The Major Parties." In *Party Democracy in Canada: The Politics of National Party Conventions,* ed. George Perlin. Toronto: Prentice-Hall Canada.

———. 1991. "Party Competition and Electoral Volatility: Canada in Comparative Perspective." In *Representation, Integration and Political*

Parties in Canada, ed. Herman Bakvis. Vol. 14 of the research studies of the Royal Commission on Electoral Reform and Party Financing. Ottawa and Toronto: RCERPF/Dundurn.

Boyle, Christine. 1983. "Home Rule for Women: Power-Sharing Between Men and Women." *Dalhousie Law Journal* 7:790–809.

Brodie, Janine. 1985. *Women and Politics in Canada.* Toronto: McGraw-Hill Ryerson.

Brodie, Janine M., and Jill M. Vickers. 1981. "The More Things Change ... Women in the 1979 Federal Campaign." In *Canada at the Polls, 1979 and 1980: A Study of the General Elections,* ed. H.R. Penniman. Washington, DC: American Enterprise Institute for Public Policy Research.

Canadian Advisory Council on the Status of Women. 1988. *Women in Politics: Becoming Full Partners.* Background paper. Ottawa: CACSW.

Carty, R. Kenneth, and Lynda Erickson. 1991. "Candidate Nomination in Canada's National Political Parties." In *Canadian Political Parties: Leaders, Candidates and Organization,* ed. Herman Bakvis. Vol. 13 of the research studies of the Royal Commission on Electoral Reform and Party Financing. Ottawa and Toronto: RCERPF/Dundurn.

Franks, C.E.S. 1987. *The Parliament of Canada.* Toronto: University of Toronto Press.

Frizzell, Alan. 1989. "The Perils of Polling." In Alan Frizzell, Jon Pammett and Anthony Westell, *The Canadian General Election of 1988.* Ottawa: Carleton University Press.

Graham, Katherine. 1990. *How Ottawa Spends: 1990–1991.* Ottawa: Carleton University Press.

Hošek, Chaviva. 1983. "Women and the Constitutional Process." In *And No One Cheered,* ed. Keith Banting and Richard Simeon. Toronto: Methuen.

Irvine, William P. 1985. "A Review and Evaluation of Electoral System Reform Proposals." In *Institutional Reforms for Representative Government.* Vol. 38 of the research studies of the Royal Commission on the Economic Union and Development Prospects for Canada. Toronto: University of Toronto Press.

Kome, Penney. 1985. *Women of Influence.* Toronto: Doubleday.

Norris, Pippa. 1987. *Politics and Sexual Equality.* Boulder: Wheatsheaf Books.

Williams, Robert. 1981. "Candidate Selection." In *Canada at the Polls, 1979 and 1980: A Study of the General Elections,* ed. H.R. Penniman. Washington, DC: American Enterprise Institute for Public Policy Research.

5

WOMEN POLITICIANS AND THEIR MEDIA COVERAGE
A Generational Analysis

Gertrude J. Robinson
Armande Saint-Jean
with the assistance of Christine Rioux

THEORETICAL SETTING

ISSUES OF GENDER, politics and the media are complexly intertwined, and their study up to now has been piecemeal. This is because gender was previously viewed as a property of individuals, rather than as a principle of social organization that systematically affects a person's behaviour and total life experience (Stacey and Thorne 1985, 307). Every step in a female politician's career, as well as the description of her political performance by the media, is therefore affected by her gender. Our study will address these interconnections and elucidate the ways in which various kinds of social barriers affect media descriptions. The interlinkages will be investigated under three headings:

- the media implications of Canadian female politicians' minority status in *all* political parties;
- the changing media coverage of women politicians from the 1950s onward; and
- future media narratives and the social challenge of women in politics.

If gender constitutes a principle of social organization, one must assume that different groups of people living in different historical periods will come to different understandings of social reality. The notion

of political generation helps to pinpoint these different understandings, because it raises questions about who, how and when these understandings were developed. Political generations have been defined in
two ways: in terms of a "life cycle" and in terms of a "cohort" (Mannheim
1952). For our purposes the "cohort" analysis is more relevant because
it addresses the issue of stability in group outlooks concerning the role
of women in public life (Knoke 1984, 192). In the case of Canadian women
politicians, these outlooks, as well as their media descriptions, changed
as the three cohorts came into contact with the developing ideas of the
women's movement.

The three different cohorts of women politicians who were active
in Canadian public life can be divided into those who served before
1970, when they were a tiny minority in provincial and federal parliaments (4.5 percent) and those who served after this time, when there
was a rapid growth in numbers. The former, our interviews show, were
born in the 1920s, while of the latter, the second generation was born
around the outbreak of the Second World War (1940s) and the third, after
1960. Each of these cohorts was thus born into a unique historical time
with its own identifiable set of media description practices.

Women politicians' historical experiences, and the social attitudes
they engendered, can be correlated with the rise of an important social
movement, "second-wave feminism," that affected the collective social
outlooks not only of North American readers and viewers but also of
the media. Sara Evans (1979) explains that the women's movement was
so important because it provided both a theory (patriarchy) and a
method (gender analysis) that radically changed women's understanding of themselves and their social roles.

The relationship between the three cohorts of women politicians
(who are differentiated by their birth dates) and their media descriptions is determined by the women's movement's understanding of itself
at the time these descriptions were made. According to Francine
Descarries and Shirley Roy (1988), the second-wave women's movement underwent three developmental changes during which its goals
were modified. In the "egalitarian reformist" stage in the 1960s, well-
educated, older professional women, as well as younger activists, spon-
taneously joined together to analyse the malaise that had "no name"
(Friedan 1963). Action and consciousness-raising groups focused on
the meaning of "equality" in the legal realm and the work place. Among
the 1960s' cohort of women politicians there were few avowed feminists,
because these women, lacking insider experience, assumed that they *were*
being treated equally. Consequently, first-cohort women politicians
focused on the implications of their own minority status and the rela-

tion of women to the state. In Canada, this decade was important because it led to the 1967 appointment of the Royal Commission on the Status of Women. This Commission, for the first time, focused attention on women's changing social role and showed that women *were* treated differentially. In its 1970 report, 166 recommendations were offered to make women more equal to men in Canadian life (Brown 1989, 143–44).

From its focus on gender equality, the women's movement in its second epoch (1970s) became radicalized and turned to issues of systematic discrimination, goaded on by student demonstrations in the United States and Europe, and the anti-war sentiments engendered by Vietnam. Feminist writers of this period began to explain women's differential social status in terms of a social and ideological system called patriarchy, which assigns women to the private sphere of the home and men to the powerful public realm of the state. In the family setting, women perform unpaid domestic labour to maintain the household economy as well as psychological services to maintain the family unit. Women's groups began to demand public-sector support for child care, and that women have control over their own bodies in regard to birth control and abortion. For second-cohort women politicians, it became clear that their minority status was not an accident, but the result of a systematic lack of recruitment into federal party structures and of access to equal party support. Consequently, they called for women's networks in all major Canadian parties and for an active search for women's participation in party caucuses and electoral campaigns.

By the beginning of the 1980s, the neo-conservative backlash that coincided with the Reagan and Thatcher regimes once again changed the emphases of North America's second-wave women's movement. With the demands for legal equality promoted by many organizations across class and gender lines (Hochschild and Machung 1990), women's groups were now focusing on various other aspects of the social and political agenda. From this period onward, it was clear that feminism did not speak with a single voice. Third-generation women politicians reflected these diversities in their own party ranks, with the Liberal and Progressive Conservative parties less open to change in structures and in personnel than the New Democratic Party. The "pluralistic feminism" of the 1980s was typical of women politicians as well as the public at large (Schneider 1988, 9). This outlook also penetrated media descriptions, which were sensitized through media-watch organizations, meetings with editors and demands from other women's groups for fairer descriptive practices.

In the 1980s, the political recruitment of women politicians reached about 20 percent, and party restructuring haltingly began. Our interviews suggest that, for the first time, a new breed of third-generation self-declared feminist politicians was being elected. In contrast to the other two cohorts, many of these women viewed politics as a career for which specific qualifications were necessary. These qualifications were not acquired through long years of party work, as before, but through scholarly, legal or business training. Militant feminists, the original trail-blazers, have vanished from the public scene as new types of leaders consolidate and extend the social equality agenda of the women's movement.

In addition to the cohort analysis, this study also incorporates a second type of analysis, the "minority" approach, to explain the differential party status of the three cohorts of women politicians. It draws attention to the fact that internal party structures and the "culture" of politics were created by men for men. They are thus neither easy to penetrate, nor comfortable to work in for women aspiring to hold office (Brodie 1985; Bashevkin 1985). Therefore, the kinds of barriers that major and minor parties place in the way of women candidates become an important index of the type of social change that has occurred since the 1950s. The three generations of women politicians that have entered politics since then have very different attitudes toward power. While we have more detailed interview material on the outlooks of the first two generations of women politicians, the third generation, which takes feminism for granted, is the most interesting to speculate about because these women will become the "new look" candidates that the Canadian public seems to be looking for in the 1990s. Their new understanding of how to organize and how to become active moulders of new people- and environment-friendly legislation will be important to contemplate in the final section of this study.

A third type of analysis that we have used in this pilot project can be loosely called a narrative analysis. In this analysis we have probed both the *context* of the media descriptions and the *patterns* these descriptions have formed. Such an analysis permits us to link the changing media portrayals of women politicians to the historical periods in which they occurred. These periods, we will show, have themselves been marked by the women's movement's changing agendas. To establish the context of media descriptions, we interviewed both male and female journalists concerning their descriptive practices, and inquired whether these were affected by gender. All of the professionals commented that they used the same descriptive practices vis-à-vis all interviewees. Women journalists however were more apt to remark that they were particularly interested in highlighting women politicians' professional backgrounds, which were rarely noted by their male colleagues.

Since this is a gender study, we began with the assumption that gender is an important descriptive characteristic that generates different kinds of narrative patterns for female and male politicians. Three different kinds of narrative styles can be distinguished: the traditional "first woman" approach, the currently used "special interest" mixed approach, and a future "egalitarian" discourse, which will invoke not gender but competence as the major characteristic by which both male and female incumbents will be judged. Time constraints precluded a general comparison of the *amount* of male and female coverage, although it would be interesting to provide this in a larger, future project. We derived our narrative patterns from a corpus of reports covering the 26 political actors we had identified in the three cohorts. This corpus comprised a total of about 250 newspaper and magazine articles distributed over a 30-year period. Each of these articles was subjected to a simple content analysis that recorded the following three characteristics: choice of adjectives, nouns and personal characteristics associated with women politicians; gender focus – type of headline used; and topics associated with women politicians. Together these characteristics provide the basis for the three kinds of generational stereotypes that we were able to isolate and that are the subject of the rest of the study.

The generational, minority and narrative analyses indicate that media descriptions are not merely *passive mirrors* of the Canadian scene, but that media institutions, and the journalists associated with them, are *active participants* in the struggle for social change. We will demonstrate how the media can, and do, through the way in which they describe public issues, retard or advance the cause and legitimacy of some groups of people and not of others. In this process, media institutions and their outlooks themselves undergo change. In the course of the past 30 years, the women's movement has been one of the major forces that, together with media-watch and consumer organizations, have drawn attention to the media's need to overcome their gender biases. As a result of these pressures, the media, which used to denigrate women's political contributions in the pre-movement era, have modified their narrative approaches in the direction of feminist demands. In spite of these changes, however, feminist analyses and their paradigms remain marginalized by the media, as the 1980s' post-feminism rhetoric indicates. Precisely because the styles of media descriptions are so important for a democratic understanding of the public world, pressures for narrative change have to be maintained until all public officials, irrespective of gender, receive the same egalitarian focus and balanced handling that social fairness in a democracy demands.

THE MEDIA IMPLICATIONS OF WOMEN'S MINORITY STATUS IN CANADIAN PARTY POLITICS

Much has been written about the minority status of women politicians in Canada, and the Royal Commission on Electoral Reform and Party Financing has heard about this issue from other researchers. Suffice it to remember, here, that at both the provincial and federal levels, the election of female representatives was insignificant until 1970. During the last two decades, however, women have made substantial gains, so that as of 1988, they represent 19.5 percent of all candidates and 13.2 percent of all federal MPs. On the provincial level, the representation of women politicians varies between an insignificant 2 percent in Newfoundland and a maximum of 22 percent in Ontario, with Quebec registering a close 19 percent. Even though these figures constitute progress for women politicians, they indicate that Canada has only about half the female political representation that is found in selected Scandinavian parliaments, such as Sweden, where 38 percent of MPs are women.

Sociologists have suggested that it takes a threshold of at least 20 to 30 percent for a minority to succeed in improving its access to a gendered profession like politics. Sweden has achieved this take-off, but even there, as Ami Lönnroth (Canada, Royal Commission 1990) mentions, the iron rule of power prevails: the greater the power, the scarcer the women. In Sweden and Canada, both department and committee chairpersons are still appointed on the basis of gender. Women have not yet penetrated the top and most powerful finance, economics or defence domains. In spite of these continuing imbalances, feminist pressures have forced health and social issues on to the public agenda, and social support for child-rearing activities is now accepted as the norm in Europe and North America (Burt et al. 1988, 142–43).

The media implications of Canadian politicians' minority status are twofold: women politicians have virtually no visibility in three of the country's 10 provinces; and successful women politicians constitute a very small subgroup of candidates available for media attention. In the next section, we will show how, due to the traditional notion that women's place is in the home, women politicians virtually disappear from the television screen. Television's electoral focus on national party leaders further reinforces the trend to ignore women in politics, because more female candidates are sponsored by minority and regional parties than by the two major parties.

Added to these gender-related obstacles caused by the political system (Burt et al. 1988, 154; Brodie and Vickers 1982, 19–22), there is a further media-specific barrier: the virtual annihilation of women in all types of television programming. Not only are there very few women represented in television programming, but women's perspectives are also left undiscussed. Tannis MacBeth-Williams et al. (1986) found that nearly two-thirds (65 percent) of all program characters were male and only one-third female. This discrepancy is further reinforced in news and public affairs coverage where 77 percent of news readers, 91 percent of experts and 70 percent of voice-overs are male (Jeffrey 1989). Women are also denigrated with respect to their capacities: they are less likely to be featured as leaders; as taking risks; or as powerful, authoritative and knowledgeable personalities.

All of these journalistic selection norms tend to make the appearance of women on the television screen rare and to feature women in their traditional secondary and home-maker roles. Only 38 percent of programs show women doing nontraditional work of *any* kind, thus reinforcing the outmoded notion that women's public place is in the "pink ghetto's" low-paying service jobs. Such norms work against the accurate description of women politicians who are engaged in a nontraditional social role. Because these norms have remained constant since the 1950s, one must conclude that the media themselves contribute to an interpretive framework that carries the implicit message that women have only a small, secondary role to play in Canadian public life (MacBeth-Williams et al. 1986).

Television's gendered framework for political reporting is reinforced by the ways in which Canada's parties function. Robert Mason Lee (1989a) argues that television as a medium has drastically changed the strategy, the conduct and the functioning of electoral campaigns. Since the early 1980s, TV has replaced the party as a campaign strategist through its news programming format and national reach. The party's strategic role has been further eroded because the media focus on the federal leaders rather than on other party personnel. Municipal and provincial contestants from smaller or new parties, which are more supportive of female candidates (Brown 1989, 150), have suffered from this changed focus. Their contestants are now rarely covered, making the real gains of women in municipal governments virtually invisible (Lavigne 1990, 55–56).

Because women are rarely selected for strategic and visible party positions, they also receive less media exposure *prior* to their candidacy. This disproportion is the outcome of two sets of gender-related party practices: women candidates have unequal access to the parties' available seats and are also disproportionately assigned to run in "lost-cause" ridings (Brodie 1985, 113–17). In the 1988 federal election, female candidates were able to contest only 45 percent of all open seats (133 out of a total of 263).

Both of these gender-related constraints have serious consequences for the media coverage of female contenders. The electronic media, with scarce personnel and a "games" approach to election coverage, associate "winning" with male politicians, while women politicians, whose campaigns are linked to lost-cause ridings, are associated with the "Flora syndrome." Sheila Copps had to contend with this association in her 1982 Ontario Liberal party leadership campaign against David Peterson. Although she garnered many votes, she was never credited with having done well in the campaign nor with having leadership potential. The scarcity of female contenders also works against women becoming visible in electoral campaigns unless their party achieves a surprise upset. Together, these gender-linked party barriers translate into additional media selection and description biases that do not apply to male politicians.

WOMEN POLITICIANS AND THEIR MEDIA COVERAGE

A third set of gender-filters that affect female, but not male, politicians arises from the unique narrative styles that the largely male reporting teams develop toward women politicians. Just as politics, until recently, was a largely male-dominated activity, so, too, has broadcast journalism been a gendered profession with traditional notions about women's place in society. A historical comparison, based on generational analysis, permits us to relate changes in styles of thought to professional reporting activities and, thus, to identify changes in reportorial styles concerning women politicians.

The Traditional Period (before 1970): Focus on "Biology"

In the period up to 1970, the general societal outlook continued to be conservative. It distinguished between the private sphere of home and family, for which women had the main responsibility, and the public sphere of politics, business and work, inhabited by men. Although the Second World War had drawn more women into the paid labour force, the ideology of the 1950s once again relegated women to their "proper" place in the home (Friedan 1963). It was not until the late 1960s that larger numbers of women, both with and without children, were drawn into the labour force to help cover the rising costs of a middle-class standard of living. At that time, as we have seen, the North American women's movement was in its infancy, and the contradictions between women's public work and private family roles were not yet well understood. This traditional role assignment provided a formidable barrier to the recruitment of women into the male domain of Canadian politics. Only 17 women politicians were elected to

Parliament in the 50 years between 1920 and 1970. Clearly, these conservative social attitudes also affected the ways in which the first generation of women politicians were narrated. Among this group were Pauline Jewett, Judy LaMarsh and Flora MacDonald.

The "traditional" narrative style, which persisted to the end of the 1960s, can generally be described as the biological approach. It uses a typification that emphasizes women qua "biologically different being," and narrates women politicians as "first woman" and "token" in the nontraditional domain of politics. As such, it perpetuates the gender stereotyping of women's activities and assumes that women politicians are primarily involved with their family and their children, and only secondarily with their political responsibilities. The notion of the restricted social role of women engenders a typification that automatically places women and their concerns into the less important "human interest" classification of public reporting. In the press, this typification places reports on female politicians into the "life-styles" section, while on television, it means that the story will appear in the final third, and therefore less important, segments of the news line-up (Robinson 1978).

The traditional topic assignment that was associated with the "first woman" approach leads male reporters to query female politicians on a restricted set of what are perceived as woman-related issues. These include social welfare, education and health. Flora MacDonald was distressed by this restricted reportorial topic assignment, a restriction that persists to this day. After the 1990 invasion of Kuwait, *The Journal* aired a "special" on the condition of foreigners detained in Iraq during which the Tehran hostage crisis was recalled. Instead of drawing on Flora MacDonald's expert knowledge as Canada's external affairs minister during that period, *The Journal* assigned the commentary roles to former ambassadors Allan Gotlieb (Washington) and Ken Taylor (Tehran).

In addition to restricting the topic assignment, which marginalizes women politicians and their interests, the traditional narrative style also focuses and frames stories in a way that undervalues women politicians' professional backgrounds and wide-ranging capacities. "First woman" reporting highlights primarily the *biological* and *family relationship* characteristics of the female politician and fails to illuminate her training and professional qualifications. Judy LaMarsh reports, in her *Memoirs of a Bird in a Gilded Cage*, that "columnists asked me about anything and everything except about my job ... My home, my cooking, my hobbies, my friends, my tastes, my likes and dislikes, all became public property to a degree suffered by none of my colleagues, including the Prime Minister [Trudeau]" (1968, 303). When women politicians are constructed as gender "tokens," they are also assumed to be under-going a great deal of role strain caused by the conflict between their political and family responsibilities. Both Flora MacDonald and Judy LaMarsh report that they were frequently asked by reporters, "Are you a politician or a woman?" as though the two were mutually exclusive.

Through the "first woman" lens, women politicians become iden-tified as the "other," as those who are "different," though their biogra-phies show that they have more in common with male politicians than with other professionals. Women politicians are equal to their male counterparts in their level of education; they have professional back-grounds in law, political science and management, and have usually worked more years in their parties and ridings (Brodie 1985, 59–60) than the male contenders. Yet, in spite of this, their *visible biological dif-ference* becomes the primary point of narrative reference. Judy LaMarsh (1968, 305) sums it up this way: "Where there are twenty-five men, the public's interest is split; when there is one woman, she becomes a focus for criticism and for curiosity."

Communications theorists have generally pointed out that media personnel, who are short of time and have restricted reportorial space, focus and condense social complexity into a series of colourful typifi-cations. These stereotypes crystallize socially accepted values and expec-tations, and change over time. Because the first generation of women politicians were viewed as playing a conflicting social role, their 1960s typifications were designed to "normalize" these perceived social con-tradictions between their biology and their social role.

Two overall strategies were used for this normalization. The first set of stereotypes – *wife of* and *family relationship designations* – make the female politician genderless. Various examples can be given of how a woman politician's "femaleness" was neutered. Women MPs like Martha Black (1935–40) and Cora Casselman (1941–45), who were *elected* to Parliament, were represented as the wife/widow, and thus as appendages of powerful husbands whose seats they had inherited. This implied that they held power not in their own right but in someone else's name. Golda Meir and Indira Gandhi, two powerful prime min-isters, in contrast, were degendered in a different way: as "grandmother Golda" and "Nehru's daughter" respectively. Their political status was lowered because their actions were viewed through a family lens.

The second set – *spinster, femme facile* and *club-woman* – all focus neg-atively on a female politician's sexual capacities. Of these, the *spinster* stereotype is most widely used for bourgeois women politicians, and it has the longest pedigree, going back to the suffragist movement of the turn of the century. This stereotype is usually applied to unmarried women of a certain age who resemble nurses or teachers and who have led a generally traditional life (Gray 1989, 19). In politics, the label "spinster" serves to describe someone who is single, has liberal ideas and is free of the obligations usually expected of a wife. Such a label incarcerates older women and subtly suggests their sexual lacunae, their inability to attract a husband. Women politicians viewed through this lens are portrayed as serious, preachy, competent and hard-working because they lack household responsibilities. The label was applied regularly to Flora MacDonald, Pat Carney, Pauline Jewett and others. Carole-Marie Allard (1987, 106) catches the negativism implied in this label: "Comments can label the woman MP. If she is a widow, she is suspected of having killed her husband. If she is divorced, she is unstable. If married, she neglects her husband, and if single, she is abnormal" [translation].

Not only were these female politicians implicitly belittled by this label, but three of them acknowledged that reporters had had the audacity to *explicitly* query them about their sex life. A male contender would have been shocked to receive such an out-of-order inquiry. Linda Goyette (1986), quoting Susan Crean, puts it well: "'The reigning notion is that if you're a man, sex comes with the territory. If you're a woman, you're expected to be celibate.'"

In the same vein, Judy LaMarsh was "neutered" by being accused of acting like a woman. Sheila Kieran (1968, 40–41) explicitly uses this strategy when she denigrates LaMarsh's career in the following words. "What was saddest about Miss LaMarsh's time in Ottawa was her style: she hit on a combination of masculine two-fistedness and a shrewd feminine guilelessness making remarks that would have earned her a sock in the mush if she had been a man. But she seemed unconsciously to understand that she could get away with it – for niggerism means making allowances for one's 'inferiors.'"

In contrast, the "femme facile" label is attached to, and stigmatizes, women politicians who do not play by the traditional social rules. By saying this, we do not mean to imply that politicians labeled in this way were exhibiting looser morals than other people of the time. What we do wish to draw attention to, however, is the fact that this label was applied to certain female politicians because they were attempting to do something unconventional. Women who were labeled in this way did not fit the "spinster" category either because they had been married or because they were still too young and too attractive to be described in this manner.

This label, like all the others, highlights a woman's gender and looks rather than her competence. The coverage of Claire Kirkland-Casgrain, who introduced the revolutionary Bill 16, giving full legal status to married women in Quebec (1964), is an excellent example of this kind of reporting. Under the headline "A striking political heroine plans to save Quebec women from their medieval bondage," Amy Booth (1964) comments, "This charming champion of women's rights, herself the first woman ever elected to the Quebec legislature, has brought two years of campaigning to a climax with a bill she describes as the first step toward first-class citizenship for Quebec women ... The lady from Jacques Cartier ... is a lot easier on the eyes than any of the current inhabitants of [Quebec's] Red Chamber."

One final label, that of the "club-woman," is applied to women politicians who espouse opinions that are in opposition to those of the male establishment (in Parliament and elsewhere) or who breach the traditional demarcations between private and public activities. Although this label is not as negative as the other two, it is by far the most tenacious put-down used to this day. It suggests that women politicians are amateurs in the public realm and that their opinions should, therefore, be disregarded. A particularly drastic example of this type of reporting is offered in Thérèse Casgrain's autobiography, where she describes a public address she gave in March 1942 to "La Société d'études et de conférences." She suggested that Quebec women become active in public life. "We will emerge from our struggle weakened if we remain turned in upon ourselves with no other horizons but those we have always known and if, led by false teachers, we remain attached to the old traditions alone" (Casgrain 1972, 106).

The publisher of *Le Bien public* of Trois-Rivières suggested that Mme. Casgrain tend to her knitting and return to her hearth. "Let her cook, sew, embroider, read, card wool, play bridge – anything rather than persist in her dangerous role of issuer of directives" (Casgrain 1972, 107).

Biology also provides the basis for gender stereotyping certain departments and portfolios that were considered socially "appropriate" for women incumbents. Women from the first generation were initially entrusted with the departments of Health (LaMarsh); Social Services (Fairclough); Citizenship and Immigration (Fairclough); and Communications (Sauvé). Lester Pearson made a "biological" classification when he found nothing wrong with ignoring the external affairs qualifications of Pauline Jewett on gender grounds. "When in 1965 Jewett expressed her dissatisfaction [at not receiving a cabinet appointment], Pearson told her; 'You know we already have a woman in the Cabinet.' 'Prime Minister,' Pauline urged, 'let's be radical. Let's have two ... or three ... or whatever!' But it was not to be" (Anderson 1987, 44). It took until the late 1970s to open up the "hard" and powerful ministries to female incumbents. Monique Bégin became minister of national revenue in 1977; Flora MacDonald, minister of external affairs in 1979; Ursula Appolloni, parliamentary secretary to the minister of defence in 1980; and Jeanne Sauvé, first female Speaker of the House of Commons in 1980.

Until the late 1960s, there were so few women politicians that they were generally perceived as the exception to the norm, as tokens in the male world of politics. Their aberrant position was picked up by the media and was reinforced in the media representations of women politicians by confusing "gender" with "sex." Media descriptions that are based on the fixed characteristics of biology erase the fact that gender is a *socially constructed* and therefore changeable set of characteristics that are anchored in the male gaze. The gender focus sets up special expectations with respect to the looks, figure, hair colour and "proper" clothing a woman politician has to wear in a particular epoch. Because these gender expectations are framed as binary opposites between the sexes, female politicians can, by definition, never *be* like men "biologically." This creates a classical double-bind situation. The confusion of sex with gender leads to some strange reportorial logic, as Peter Gzowski's (1962) generally laudatory article about Judy LaMarsh and Pauline Jewett demonstrates. In it he concludes that if the two politicians remain elected, the "caucuses of the future will feel the effect of two strong and lively feminine voices. The ideas those voices present won't [however] be feminine at all" (ibid., 52). An even more drastic effect of the sex/gender confusion is found in a 1962 article in which *feminine* behaviour requirements, rather than the mandate of her portfolio, are the substance of a report about Immigration Minister Ellen Fairclough. The article, entitled "Un ministre bien chapeauté," notes:

> Our immigration minister Mrs. Ellen Fairclough travels, meets people and wears a hat much more often than do the majority of Canadians. Since becoming a federal cabinet minister in 1957, Mrs. Fairclough has travelled some 240 000 miles, mostly in Canada, and has worn more than three dozen hats. The functions she has attended over the last four years have permitted her to wear several styles of headgear that are not specifically feminine. While flying, she wore a helmet used by pilots for protection in case of accidents [translation].
> (*La Presse* 1962)

Such a narrative construction systematically erases women's contributions to the public sphere, and also types these contributions as less important solely because they have been made by women.

The Transitional Period (1970–90): Focus on Power

In the 20 years between 1970 and 1990, political scientists point out, the public view of women's social role has changed. Three occurrences contributed to this change in social outlook: the Royal Commission Report on the Status of Women tabled in 1970; the changing market requirements of the post-industrial society; and the growth and radicalization of the women's movement in the last two decades. Although the research reports prepared for the Commission created a substantial backlash among conservative women, they enabled the Commission to make over 160 recommendations to ensure that women would have legal equality in Canadian public life (Kieran 1968, 42). Included in these recommendations was the call for parties to recruit more women into politics.

The post-industrial economy, with its multiplication of service jobs, precipitated the widespread entry of married women (68 percent) and mothers (54 percent) into the labour market and coined the concept of the "working mother." Women's experiences outside the home led to calls for pay equality in the workplace throughout the 1970s and initiatives for legal equity in the 1980s, when the *Canadian Charter of Rights and Freedoms* in its initial version omitted this section (Burt et al. 1988, 140–41). The 1979–82 Charter debate, furthermore, sensitized women's groups to the facts that contact with men in politics would not automatically lead to constitutional input and that social and political change needed concerted action from female legislators and grassroots lobbying from women's groups (Hošek 1989, 507).

Of the three factors bringing about greater acceptance of women's role in public life, the women's movement must be credited with having had the greatest impact. It addressed the mismatch between work opportunities opening up for women in the 1970s and prevailing conservative views about how women *ought* to behave. In doing so, it provided an overarching and systemic explanation of women's secondary status. During the 1970s, feminist theorists developed an understanding of patriarchy and discovered that it was present in all societies. These theorists also documented that patriarchy took different forms in different historical epochs and in different countries. As a universal system, however, patriarchy always has the characteristic of excluding women from the prestigious professions (including politics and the media) and the top jobs.

During the 1980s, the widespread diffusion of feminism's equality agenda across social class and gender brought feminism to the attention of everyone and generated grassroots activities by diverse women's groups on diverse social issues having to do with reproduction, widely defined. Anna Coote and Polly Pattullo (1990, 77) define reproduction not only as "child-bearing and rearing, but [as] all the work that goes into sustaining human life in the family and the community."

The support for women's legal equality led to qualified public acceptance of women's role in the political sphere. Although there is as yet little proactive support for women candidates in the Liberal and Conservative parties, the NDP introduced gender-related criteria into its party operations and the selection of convention delegations in the 1970s (Brown 1989, 144). The number of women politicians has grown to about 20 percent in at least three provincial legislatures and to an average of 20 to 30 percent in municipal governments in Canada's major cities (Vancouver, Toronto, Montreal and Halifax) (Lavigne 1990, 5; Maillé 1990, 14). These figures indicate that since the 1980s, women legislators are coming close to the "take-off" point where a minority can begin to effect institutional change, at least on the municipal level.

Two additional factors have profoundly influenced women's political power in both the United States and Canada. The first was a change in women's electoral participation, the second, a voting differentiation between women and men. Together these became known as the "gender gap." In the United States, the differential voter turnout, which amounted to 10 percent in favour of men in 1950, has been reversed – by 1984 women had a 7 percent lead over men in voter participation (Mueller 1988b, 22).

In Canada, Janine Brodie (1985, 126) noted a similar numerical shift in favour of women, and additionally discovered that, by 1983, women preferred the Liberal party by a margin of 10 percent. Flora MacDonald confirmed that all parties in the 1984 election campaign took this gender gap extremely seriously, because it seemed to suggest that women were voting as an interest group. To capture women voters, the Conservatives asked Flora MacDonald to lead "consciousness-raising" sessions for Conservative MPs, while Sheila Copps and other Liberal party women were asked to advise John Turner. He proved as unenlightened as many of his parliamentary colleagues about the government's role in women's quest for equality (Copps 1986, 156–57). Because both parties had constructed the same platforms for attracting women voters the gender gap was invisible in 1984. This does not mean, however, that women and their special interests have disappeared from the political agenda. The candidates' debate, organized by Chaviva Hošek, who was National Action Committee (NAC) president at the time, indicates that *all* parties will have to address women's social and peace agendas in the future.

The transitional narrative approach, with its focus on power, reflects a period in which social and journalistic values are in flux. Old attitudes toward women clash with newer "equality" values; at the same time, women are visibly rising toward middle-level power positions in both the political and the media realms. During this period, therefore, the coverage of women politicians and their activities has moved from the back to the front pages of newspapers, and female anchors are beginning to interview the growing number of female legislators and ministers in a more even-handed manner. But topic selection and narrative frames concerning women politicians *still* remain differentiated from those of male incumbents.

The second set of stereotypes, which crystallized in the 1970s and 1980s, has been profoundly influenced by the ideology of feminism, which has forced women politicians and others to take a position on women's social identity. As we have seen, feminist research throughout the period identified the nature and origins of the nonsymmetrical power relations between the genders and also surveyed the barriers to women's egalitarian progress in the male worlds of business, the top professions and the media (Robinson 1975; Crean 1987). Even after 20 years of training and experience, the "glass ceiling" has not been breached by female managers in most media organizations. Nowadays, women make up only 9 percent of editors-in-chief and 6 percent of managing editors in the Canadian Daily Newspaper Publishers Association. Furthermore all 33 people promoted to senior management jobs in 1989 were male (Cornacchia 1990). The situation is no better in television and film production, where, according to an American study by the National Commission on Working Women, "women made up 15 percent of producers, 25 percent of writers and 9 percent of directors of shows aired in 1990. In prime-time shows women held 43 percent of the roles but were rarely depicted at all after age 40" (*Gazette*, 1990).

These figures indicate that it remains difficult to integrate a pro-woman perspective into media descriptions and that anti-egalitarian attitudes toward women remain pervasive in Canadian society and in Canadian newsrooms. The four new stereotypes incorporate these ambivalences, although they frame female politicians in a power network, which is superficially more complimentary. Another stylistic characteristic that we found for this period is the fact that all of the stereotypes are *inflected* by a feminist discourse and by feminist social expectations. Our analyses will show that journalists use this discourse in two very different ways: either as a simple *classificatory* device or as an *interest group* argument. As a classificatory device, the label feminist is attached to an individual female politician and used as though it describes a type of party membership. When it denotes an interest group, it implies that women *as a group* have gained political power and influence that is somehow illegitimate. In both uses, the "feminist" designation is shunned by women politicians, who dislike the negative connotations of the "new F-word," as Charlotte Gray calls it (1989, 19).

First, the most spectacular and most visible of the new stereotypes is that of the *superwoman*. It is applied to a young, intelligent, active and ambitious woman who succeeds on "all levels" and "has it all." She combines a family with her career, and she is as groomed as she is competent in her ministerial responsibilities. The superwoman is a hybrid: she embodies both traditional characteristics (family and children) with the modern traits of the businesswoman (superior IQ, enormous capacities for work, an iron constitution as well as charm and generosity). Arlie Hochschild and Anne Machung (1990) describe the superwoman's advertising image as the woman with the flowing blond hair, attaché case in one hand and a child in the other. Canadian politicians described in this manner are Liza Frulla-Hébert, Sharon Carstairs, Chaviva Hošek, Iona Campagnolo and Janice Johnson. Hubert Bauch (1982) of the Montreal *Gazette* applies this narrative style to Iona Campagnolo: "Iona Campagnolo has been an instinctive climber all her life ... From the time she blew into Ottawa eight years ago, like a refreshing, scented breeze off the western sea, Campagnolo has been tagged as a contender for the whole bag of marbles ... As if to prove them right she made it into the cabinet [in] less than two years ... She was bright, articulate and a looker with a slightly intimidating touch of class. She was Iona, 'La Camp' ... who had clawed her way 'from cannery row to Parliament Hill.'"

The feminist version of the superwoman is offered in this description of Janice Johnson as reported by Val Sears (1983) in the *Toronto Star*: "When Janice Johnson, national director of the Progressive Conservative party, was a kid at college in Winnipeg she was sort of radical ... Today, Janice Johnson is 37, tidier, and running a party and her life conservatively, stylishly, but still with that red stripe setting off the blue. As the Conservative party's chief executive, [she is] an apparatchik with her manicured hands on the strings. She is also a feminist in a nest of Tory male chauvinists."

The second of the four stereotypes for narrating women politicians is that of the champion. This narrative approach is close to that of the superwoman, but tends to be applied to women politicians "of a certain age" who have led a more traditional life. Often a woman narrated in this way has come to politics after she has proved herself in another domain, perhaps business, sports or various charitable organizations. Her children are usually older, and her family obligations more compatible with her public representation duties. She, too, pays attention to her grooming, is open to the media and aware of her previous accomplishments. Among the politicians who have earned this classification are Pat Carney, Monique Landry, Monique Vézina, Lucie Pépin and Margaret Thatcher. Under the headline "Tough Woman Tory Has Skill To Be Party Leader, Next PM," the Montreal *Gazette* (1975) comments, "The right honorable Margaret Thatcher, 49, is no ordinary woman: that she is being even seriously considered as the next leader of the Conservative Party, a body with more than its fair share of male chauvinists, is in itself a remarkable achievement. Those who have worked with her ... have no doubt that she has the ability to be ... leader ... She has stamina and talent. Her appetite for work is prodigious. She enjoys making decisions. Thatcher is tough, not ruthless." By 1976, she had earned the "Iron Lady" epithet from the Soviet Army newspaper *Red Star*, which, according to an interview, she did not mind because it well represented her outlook on politics (*Maclean's* 1990, 41).

Margaret Thatcher's counterpart, the "feminist" champion, is Lucie Pépin. Her coverage reveals many of the collective themes that make up this image. But she is narrated with greater warmth by Leslie Fruman (1984) in the *Toronto Star*.

> On being a feminist in 1984, Lucie Pépin has a cool-down approach. She's been called a male-oriented feminist, and says women have to be ready to work with men to help the advancement of women ... The elegant but tough former president of the Canadian Advisory Council on the Status of Women might offend the feminist establishment with words like those ... Her father wanted her to go to medical school, but Pépin opted to train as a nurse ... [because] she wanted to be free to get married ... It was her work in nursing that taught her the valuable lessons that put her in contact with issues facing women.

The third label we encountered in our analyses is one we have called being *one of the boys*. This narrative scheme is applied to women politicians who have been accepted into the ranks by the male political establishment, which counts them as part of the "gang." This type of female politician adopts a "masculine" stance in politics, which means either that she does not resort to what are called "feminine wiles" to achieve her goals (charm, coquetry, wheedling) or that she accepts and operates by the conventional rules of the game. Women politicians who are "one of the boys" benefit from this kind of acceptance but are, at the same time, continually reminded that they are an anomaly and may be placed in the unenviable position of being used as an alibi *against* women's interests. Examples are legion, such as the woman minister who had to bail out the reputation of a male colleague who had made an unpardonably sexist remark in a constituency speech. Or the situation where the first female Justice Minister was appointed just as anti-abortion legislation (Bill C-43) was being re-introduced. This narrative approach has been applied, among others, to Barbara McDougall, Mary Collins, Kim Campbell, Lorna Marsden and Sheila Copps. In Collins' case, Charlotte Gray (1989) has the following to say about the new female recruits to the Progressive Conservative party:

> They exuded sisterly solidarity ... Mary Collins, the bubbly member from BC, now associate minister of national defence and co-host of the party, groaning about her kid's untidiness. There was ... Marjory LeBreton, number two in the Prime Minister's Office ... Finally, the sibling superior of the PC sisterhood strode through the door ... Barbara McDougall, minister for the status of women and minister of employment and immigration. The most striking characteristic of the party, however, was the murmured distaste for anything that smacked of "feminism". Tactics borrowed from the women's movement may have steered the newcomers into the Tory harbour but its ideology left many of them cold. They wanted to join the political system, not change it. "Why do the press insist on treating women as a special interest group?" snapped Diana Togneri of Montreal. (Gray 1989, 17–18)

In contrast to the women politicians who consider feminism the "second F-word," Sheila Copps is outspokenly upbeat about being described as "one of the gang" and as a feminist. In her autobiographical *Nobody's Baby*, she says, "I take pride in being a feminist. Look at the word itself; it comes from the Latin *femina*, woman; and being a woman is cause enough for being proud. I take pride, too, in representing my constituency – not only the riding which sent me to Parliament, but my larger constituency, the women of Canada" (1986, 89).

A *Maclean's* article narrates her leadership campaign in the following manner: "*Sheila Copps*: As the most vocal member of the Liberal 'Rat-Pack' – a small group of MPs known for their aggressive Question Period attacks during the Conservative government's first term – Copps earned a reputation among her Tory opponents as a shrill firebrand ... Advisers to the 37-year-old MP for Hamilton East say that Copps's campaign will highlight her youth, gender and populist style. She has proven her appeal once before, finishing second to David Peterson in the Ontario Liberal leadership race in 1982" (Kaihla 1990, 28).

The final set of stereotypes that frame women politicians is the familiar *wife of* designation. It is a narrative scheme that we have already encountered in the description of first-generation politicians. This stereotype's survival into the 1980s may be a result of the fact that it has been applied to such high-profile women leaders as Corazon Aquino of the Philippines and Violetta Ciamorro of Nicaragua. In Canada, however, it has been given a new twist. Where it was earlier applied to "amateur" wives or daughters of politicians who had taken over their husband's or father's seats in the legislature, it is now applied as well to wives who have previous political or professional experience. Two cases in point are Jeanne Sauvé and Maureen McTeer. Norman Laplante (1990) clearly highlights the marital connection and uses it as the organizing principle for an article: "Throughout their respective careers in Canadian public life, Jeanne and Maurice Sauvé have shown a keen desire to work for the cause of national unity. The first Canadian couple to be admitted to the Privy Council, they were at the forefront of the Canadian political scene for over twenty years."

A similar narrative scheme organizes the coverage of Maureen McTeer, who ran as Conservative candidate in Carleton–Gloucester (Ottawa) in 1988. In this case, however, the "wife of" label is used to denigrate the candidate's considerable competence through a barrage of innuendo concerning the supposed advantages she gained from her husband's political position. Robert Mason Lee, in a 1989 *Saturday Night* article entitled "Sorry Mo," attacks McTeer's column in *Chatelaine* magazine, and McTeer for failing to divulge that her columnist status had been achieved because of her marital connection.

In contrast to the first set of stereotypes – *spinster, femme facile, club-woman* and *wife of* – which have to do with the *traditional social roles* of women, the four new stereotypes, applied to the second generation of women politicians during the 1970s and early 1980s, are constructed around the "power game." The *superwoman* achieves in both the private and the public spheres of activity. The *champion* is accomplished in such activities as business, professional or benevolent organizations. The members of the *gang* have learned the rules of the political game and use them like a man. The only stereotype that harks back to those used on the first generation of women politicians is the "wife of" label. But even this is now narrated with a different twist, an acknowledgement that it is appropriate for *both* spouses to have careers. In the 1980s, after all, two-career families are more prevalent than the male-headed household.

Public narrations recreate and incorporate social changes, not like passive mirrors but like active prisms through which our public understandings are fashioned. In spite of the fact that the recent set of stereotypes narrate women politicians in a power-game context, they still fail to evaluate women's political competence in career terms. Instead women are judged on their personal ability to play by the masculine rules of the political game. These include personal aggressiveness, adversarial performance in Question Period, hard-headedness and coolness under fire. Readers are told approvingly that Sheila Copps and Sharon Carstairs are more aggressive than their male counterparts. Such evaluative criteria continue to use the male species as the norm and to construct the female as the exception, the secondary, thus leaving the unbalanced social hierarchy intact.

With a shift in the stereotyping of women politicians came an associated shift in how feminism is treated by the media. In the 1970s, the media discovered feminism for its "novel" and "sensational" characteristics, as having something to do with changing language and changing lifestyles. Media practitioners generally simplified the reporting of this widespread social movement by turning feminism into an *individual characteristic*, similar to an organizational membership. The media then used the label "women's lib" for easy classification of feminists. Through this interpretation, the *movement* aspects of feminism were erased and disappeared from public sight. The media consequently concluded, by the middle of the decade, that the women's movement was dead and that the 1980s were the post-feminist era. Such reasoning has no basis in social fact, as even the media people now know. But this interpretation served as a convenient alibi for ignoring women's increased municipal and regional initiatives, as well as the networking that has occurred outside of the state sector.

In the early 1980s, the American media discovered a gender gap in the Reagan election, and by the 1984 campaign, the Progressive Conservatives knew that this gap might affect Canadian women voters as well. Consciousness-raising activities, as we have seen, were undertaken by first-generation women politicians in their party caucuses, and these activities were picked up by the media. By 1987, a Decima poll confirmed that there was a three-point male/female difference in voting preference, and that the Tories were particularly disliked by working women (only 28 percent would vote Conservative) (Gray 1989, 18). A computer-assisted program to reach a riding's undecided voters through customized letters saved the Tories in 1987, and the gender gap failed to materialize once more (Lee 1989a). The media had, however, learned their lesson and began to report feminist groups as a potential lobby with the power to change the political rules.

This reportorial stance became a prominent aspect of the coverage of Audrey McLaughlin's December 1989 leadership win over Dave Barrett in Winnipeg. The two reasons that were immediately offered for Audrey McLaughlin's NDP convention success were her gender and her feminist support, *not* her varied professional credentials such as her social work background, her experience with community organizations in the Yukon or her Third-World engagement. Both the "sex" and "feminist" themes, as we have seen, have been used to describe and subtly put down women politicians for not being men throughout the 1980s. The *Globe and Mail's* (1989) Jeffrey Simpson points out that it was McLaughlin's sex that got her elected:

> From the moment Ms McLaughlin declared her candidacy, she became the New Democrat to beat for one simple, compelling and ultimately decisive reason – her sex ... For seven consecutive elections, the NDP has been mired in the rut of 15 to 20 per cent of the national vote. Maybe a woman leader, wondered many New Democrats, would produce a larger number of voters. For the women who supported Ms McLaughlin, it was time for the political system to confront fully the whole matrix of women's issues through the symbolic message sent by the election of a female leader.

Hugh Winsor (1989), another *Globe and Mail* columnist, adds the second theme: a "feminist" network had helped her to win over Dave Barrett, when it may, in fact, have been her *campaign organization:* "Ms McLaughlin had by far the largest number of workers (many borrowed from the feminist movement), headquarters in each province and territory, and a computerized delegate tracking system that gave her floor captains up-to-the-minute print-outs on each riding's delegates."

A day or two later, Dalton Camp (1989) in the *Toronto Star* elaborated on the "feminist" connection, suggesting that it was somehow illegal for a candidate to have a women's network to support her bid for the leadership:

> Pauline Jewett, mother hen to the feminist cause, put the issue squarely before the Canadian people through the radio facilities of the Mother Corporation: There was sexism in the media. Speaking from the convention scene in Winnipeg, Pauline said (I wrote this down) she had noticed a lot of "criticism of Audrey (McLaughlin) because she's a woman" ... I thought the NDP convention suffered from an excess of feminist militancy at the barricades. Against the militants stood the

rest of the delegates, as though barefoot on a floor of ground glass, weighing each word, idiom, and simile on the gender scale. (Reprinted with permission. The Toronto Star Syndicate)

Five days later, on 9 December 1989, Peggy Curran of the Montreal *Gazette* offered McLaughlin's response to the gender accusation: "If the newcomer from the North finished first at the NDP convention in Winnipeg, critics said, her gender would be the only explanation. Friends and supporters say the 53-year-old member of Parliament for Yukon handled the charges of tokenism with her customary wit. Dropping in on campaign workers at the two-storey log cabin 'Yukon skyscraper' that houses her Whitehorse office, McLaughlin said: 'Well, I thought about running as a man, but I decided against it.'"

On the same day (9 December 1989), Graham Fraser in the *Globe and Mail* confronted and illustrated the condescending coverage of McLaughlin in the "View from the Hill":

The reporter smiled indulgently and asked the leader of the New Democratic party her first question after she had made her first address to the House of Commons as leader. "Audrey, tell me," he said, "Were your knees shaking when you stood up[?]" "No. No," she said firmly and flatly. "Really. I've been in Question Period before." ... As the first woman to lead a Canadian federal party, Ms McLaughlin still seemed to be subject to a different kind of scrutiny on Wednesday. One reporter inquired about the mark on her cheek ...; a national columnist noted that she had worn a green silk dress on her first day as NDP leader ... One of the women reporters within earshot did a double-take when the NDP leader was asked if her knees had been shaking. "Give me a break," she muttered. "Do you think that will be his first question to Paul Martin if he becomes Liberal leader?"

The charges and countercharges traded among print reporters indicate that the media establishment is as unprepared as the political establishment to admit a new female player *on her merits* into the game of high-stakes politics. Whether Audrey McLaughlin will become a great leader of Canada's NDP remains an open question. What is not open, however, is her right to be taken seriously by the press. Rosemary Brown (1989, 171) found that when the press could no longer trivialize her 1975 NDP leadership bid, "there was a subtle shift away from superficial discussions of my 'elegance,' 'private school education,' and 'home in the fashionable Point Grey district of Vancouver' to more thoughtful and serious speculation as to the potential effect of my candidacy on the New Democratic Party and on Canada."

FUTURE MEDIA NARRATIVES AND THE POLITICAL CHALLENGE OF WOMEN

Media Narratives of Women Politicians: Differential Approach

In spite of an evolution of stereotypes concerning women politicians and their contributions to statesmanship, any form of stereotypical writing focuses on a set of *reductive* characteristics that severely limit the details and points of view a text is able to express. The fact that older stereotypes, which characterized the first generation of women politicians primarily in terms of their biological difference (spinster, femme facile) and their social relations to men (wife, grandmother, granddaughter), have been replaced by new ones, does not constitute progress in itself. The bio-social focus of the pre-1960s period depicted the first generation of women politicians as either adventurers or tokens. As adventurers, they had escaped from their "proper" domestic sphere and therefore wielded a different and lesser kind of power than that held by men. As tokens, women's presence was used as proof that minimal openings for "exceptional" women existed in the male domain of politics. In such a narrative frame, women's political contributions are underestimated and marginalized because they are portrayed as exceptions to the socially defined female norms, and the women themselves lose their competence and credibility when they are portrayed as biologically strange "birds in a gilded cage," as Judy LaMarsh tellingly described her political existence.

Even the transitional stereotypes, although seemingly different and more modern, remain restrictive because they refer to power in the public realm. While media reports reflect the liberalized view that women *can* be integrated into the political realm, the labels indicate that such integration is only possible for certain types of women politicians. Acceptable women politicians are the *superwoman*, who performs superbly in both her private and her public roles; the *champion*, who shares a similar background with her male colleagues (business, sports, professions); and the *gang* member, who has learned, and employs, the male rules of the political game. One additional label, the *wife of*, is a carry-over from the past, but is now remodeled as a husband's "junior partner" in a dual-career family.

The transitional narrative strategies applied to second- and third-generation politicians who are marked as feminist or non-feminist by the media, indicate that there is much greater resistance to, and worry about, feminist demands for women's social equality in the 1980s than there was in the 1970s. No wonder such inventions as the "post-feminist era" or the "death of the women's movement" are proclaimed by journalists, although the sociological evidence does not corroborate these interpretations. Some journalists and politicians would like to silence feminist demands for completion of the social revolution, which guarantees women and other minorities access to the public domain. The transitional narrative approaches incorporate a deep-seated ideological ambivalence concerning women's changing social identity. While egalitarian principles promoted by women's groups remain the ideal, a majority of politicians and media personnel have difficulty accommodating women's demands for power-sharing. In such a situation, the conservative backlash against feminism in the Reagan and Mulroney eras must be interpreted as a defensive reaction to women's advances in the public realm.

The reportage of Audrey McLaughlin's leadership win graphically indicates that the majority of media people are just as unaccustomed as most politicians to the appearance of women in the halls of Parliament or in ministerial chairs. Sheila Copps (1986, 38) notes that, as late as the 1982 Ontario leadership campaign, "the press and the party establishment were nowhere near as liberated as the average voting delegate" concerning the candidacy of a woman. This ambivalence is still reflected in both the reasons given for McLaughlin's win (her sex and feminist group support) and the types of questioning she underwent after her first appearance as NDP leader. The fact that women politicians cannot yet be credited with wearing the mantle of power without belittling commentary indicates that "women's political past, like our political future continues to be contested ground" for interpretation (Vickers 1989, 18).

Our generational analysis shows that neither the old (up to the 1960s) nor the transitional (1970s and 1980s) narrative prisms reflect much of what constitutes the social reality and political experience of contemporary Canadian women. Female political leaders, representatives and political women in general feel uncomfortable with, and unwelcome in, parliamentary settings designed by nation-building brotherhoods, who are implacably proprietorial of women (Coote and Pattullo 1990, 274). The major lacunae of the transitional discourse require only summary attention because they have already been discussed. The existing stereotypical narrative conventions treat political women and men very differently. Both the narrative focuses and the evaluative criteria for the two genders are at variance. Four narrative focuses are applied only to women. These focuses:

- tend to ignore the substance of a female incumbent's speeches in favour of her personal characteristics (looks, dress, hair);
- fail to give recognition for prior political activities, with the result

that no one knows the stages in a woman's political career, which
together signify her "competence";

- make women politicians responsible for women *as a class* when
  gender is known to be only one of many factors in interest-group
  formation; and
- use "feminism" to denote a negative personal characteristic, and
  thus erase the group dimensions of this diversified social movement.

The evaluative criteria are also at variance for women and men:

- Women have to live up to a considerably higher standard of excellence than do men.
- The political performance of women is judged only by the extremes
  of the scale (good and bad), while men are evaluated across the
  whole scale, including the mediocre middle range.
- Women politicians have to live up to a moral code of sexual absten-
  tion not imposed on men.

These differential narrative focuses and evaluative criteria raise a
series of questions. Among these are the following: To what extent do
the media adequately perceive the difference in attitudes, goals and
understandings that motivate female and male politicians? Why are
women drawn in greater numbers to local, municipal and regional
activity than to provincial and national political involvement? How
adequate is the picture that the media construct of the political arenas
in which women prefer to operate? And even more fundamentally, is
there any difference in the motivations that propel women and men into
political life? Since the media provide society with the words and concepts
for naming and constructing social and political reality, how adequately
are they performing this task for women and women's concerns? The
veracity and accuracy with which the media represent women politicians and their views are inextricably linked to the effectiveness with
which political women can shape their society. Conversely, inaccurate
and elliptical media descriptions deprive both female representatives
and citizens of their voice and their input into the public domain.

There is evidence today that women readers and viewers are deeply
troubled by the restrictive media reporting of modern women's social
concerns and by the irrelevance of many media reports to their common
life experience. Recent analyses confirm that newspapers, which supply their readers with an overwhelmingly white, male, middle-class
view of the world, have lost 25 percent of their female readership in

the past decade (Cornacchia 1990; Walker 1990). These kinds of evidence indicate that women have different notions about the nature of political activity, and that they are becoming alienated from Canada's governing bodies such as Parliament and the Senate. Our own interviews document that women politicians feel uncomfortable operating in the "boys' school" atmosphere of these institutions and come to politics with different expectations. Women politicians also complain that media journalists and politicians alike are unaware of and mistrust the female networks and female solidarity which women's groups of all kinds have generated around women's issues. Many of these women's groups have been labelled "feminist" according to Chaviva Hošek, although the majority are in fact traditional women's organizations that lend their support to feminist causes at certain times. Among these are voluntary organizations (like the Canadian Federation of University Women); groups providing specific services to women (rape crisis centres, etc.); advisory councils to the government (like the Canadian Advisory Council on the Status of Women); and specialized national voluntary associations that lobby in areas of their particular expertise (such as the National Association of Women and the Law) (Hošek 1989, 494–96).

The Challenge of Women in Canadian Politics

The women's movement theory of patriarchy and the method of gender analysis have played a crucial role in North American women's understanding of their social world in the 1990s and mobilized them by keeping them aware of the continued existence of sexual inequalities (Norris 1988, 233). In addition, they have alerted researchers that traditional theories of politics are unable to encompass many of women's political activities. New theories must go beyond the conventional political science focus on state institutions and élite politics to incorporate the experiences of grassroots organizers, who have learned to operate within and outside of male-dominated institutions (Vickers 1989, 22). Our interviews, and those of others who have talked to women politicians in Great Britain and Germany (Lepsius 1990, 68), confirm that "Parliament is more than an institution of ancient mystique and obscure language; it is a place made by men for men, and still fiercely ruled by them. Women have been admitted, but their presence is acceptable only if they do not draw attention to themselves as women, and only if they divest themselves of any uniquely female preoccupation such as motherhood" (Coote and Pattullo 1990, 256).

Similar views have been expressed by Canadian politicians like Rosemary Brown (NDP), Sheila Copps (Liberal) and others who have remarked on the isolation of their "token" status. In her autobiography

Nobody's Baby, Sheila Copps (1986, 28) has the following to say about her experiences in the Ontario caucus: "My colleagues were gracious and friendly, but clearly saw me as an ornament to the party – nice to have around as long as I knew my place. One of the ironies was that most of the men in caucus thought I enjoyed the publicity ... Some were even resentful when I had anything worthwhile to say. Every time I would rise in question period, one of my colleagues would mutter under his breath: 'There goes Sheila. The cameras are rolling again.' What he didn't realize was that ... I felt isolated and out of place" (as one among thirty-three).

Ordinary women, too, feel alienated from élite politics as it is generally practised. They have overwhelmingly organized themselves at the grassroots level in order to achieve better housing conditions, recreation for disadvantaged children or battered women's shelters. A political activist explains her alienation this way: "I went to a lot of meetings and listened to the people talking. They weren't talking about what I was even interested in ... They were talking about the wages struggle all the time, about trade-union issues, and I thought, they never talk about housing issues or what are we to do with the kids, stuff like that" (Coote and Pattullo 1990, 50). Coote and Pattullo comment that, when asked about politics, women felt that the fabric of their lives was not a "proper" concern of politics. No wonder so many women feel that politics has nothing to do with them.

Although the isolation of élite women politicians has become less pronounced as a result of the 1984 and 1988 elections, their numbers are not yet large enough to enable them to influence federal politics. In the 1980s, women gained access as "helpers" in what scientist Ursula Franklin describes as the political "sandbox," but they are as yet denied the proper tools for the job (Jeffrey 1990, 73). The picture looks a bit better on the provincial level where 20 percent of legislators are now women, but the most significant advances have been made in the municipal administrations of Canada's largest and medium-sized cities: there, women number one-third of all representatives. This higher proportion of women's representation at the municipal level of government is a function of the fact that this kind of political service can be combined with family responsibilities. In the 1990s, we can expect not only that women will become firmly entrenched in Canadian political life but also that they will be increasingly able to influence the types and outcomes of legislation. It is additionally plain that the greatest political innovations in the coming decade will originate from municipal experiences.

With these developments in mind, is there any evidence that more women politicians will make a difference to the Canadian political scene? Do they have different motives, attitudes and goals, and thus diversify the points of view from which the political sandboxes of the future will be constructed? Accumulated research from a variety of sources, and our own conversations with representatives from the three generations of women politicians, indicate that women do seem to have different reasons for running for political office. They also conceive of political power in variant ways. And, furthermore, their understandings of social interaction differ from those espoused by their male colleagues. These differences add up to a differential political profile and a different agenda for women politicians that seems to be perceived by, and gives them an edge with, the Canadian electorate.

In response to our inquiries concerning their reasons for running for political office, the overwhelming majority of women of all three generations, including nonfeminist and feminist candidates, said that they were seeking office in order to improve the conditions of human life. Among the conditions mentioned were the rectification of social violence, racism and the plights of minorities. European evidence confirms that, in Great Britain and Germany, too, social involvement is a strong mobilizing force (Grewe-Partsch 1990, 48). Jill Vickers (1989, 20) explains that what she calls the "service-based" conception of politics has deep roots in the first-wave suffragist movement. First-wave women placed a high value on citizenship, which incorporated both the Christian duty to help others and the concepts of self-help and community building. In contrast, many male candidates view the business of entering national politics as a profession or a career that demands few special qualifications and relatively little expertise while providing them with middle-class status. It is well known that men are educated and trained for career building in ways that women are not. Yet, the political establishment is not yet ready to grant second- and third-generation women incumbents with impressive arrays of qualifications a place in politics (Brodie 1985, 59). One reason why these qualifications are rarely public knowledge, our evidence shows, is that most media reporting does not mention or give women credit for them.

A second characteristic that distinguishes female from male politicians is their attitude toward power. This difference in attitude was noted by Denise Falardeau during the Royal Commission–sponsored symposium in Montreal (Canada, Royal Commission 1990). Here Falardeau noted that women politicians she knew looked for power, but not at any price and not in general. Women tended to look for power to do something concrete. For many women politicians power is an instrument rather than an object in itself. Thérèse Lavoie-Roux echoes this sentiment in an interview with Marie-Jeanne Robin (1983, 177–78).

She responds: "I cannot answer that. But so far I remain convinced that women do not want power for the sake of power ... I don't think we have the same code of ethics" [translation].

Rosemary Brown (1989, 228) expands on this difference in her autobiography *Being Brown* by making a useful distinction between "hierarchical power," which is based in a bureaucracy, and "personal power," which arises from collective decision making. In assessing her 14-year provincial NDP career in various Vancouver ridings (1972–86), she says:

> I was actually very disappointed by how little real power I had and how often I failed to live up to the expectations of people who appealed to me for help.
>
> At first I thought that if I had been a cabinet minister I could have had some direct power, but even of that I'm not sure; often cabinet ministers were forced to introduce and defend legislation to which they were opposed, because it was the will of the leader, majority vote in caucus or recommendation of the party pollsters ... In retrospect, I realize that it was power in the traditional patriarchal context that I lacked, rather than the more personal and compelling power that comes from collective decision-making and the mutual respect people of like mind share with each other. (© 1989 by Rosemary Brown. Reprinted by permission of Random House of Canada Ltd.)

However, personal power alone is no match for hierarchical team-based power, through which high-ranking bureaucrats or ministerial advisers can, and do, affect legislative decision making. In these bureaucratic behind-the-scenes realms, women continue to be underrepresented (Brown 1989, 232). Yet, even here people are feeling the 1990s' winds of change. A number of our respondents mentioned that the resistance to women politicians was strongest in one particular stratum, which Sheila Copps (1986, 43) dubbed the "MUPPIES" – male urban professional party workers who view women as a threat to their traditional hold over Canada's party system.

A final distinction between female and male politicians concerns their attitudes toward social interaction and its norms. As "outsider-insiders," minority politicians tend to find that it is more useful to play a catalytic rather than an exclusionary role. Maureen McTeer (Canada, Royal Commission 1990) echoed these sentiments in her presentation to the Montreal symposium where she advocated the need for a less hierarchical and exclusionary communication style in Parliament. Ami Lönnroth (ibid.), a Swedish representative at the symposium, pointed out that women, through their increased labour-force participation, were carrying the conciliatory approach into the realms of industry and business merely by being there. It was time they did the same in legislative councils.

Pauline Jewett confirmed this interpretation in our interview; she noted that Audrey McLaughlin, as NDP leader, was operating in a consensus style in her caucus, following in the steps of Pearson, Stanfield and Douglas. As a result, Jewett mused, McLaughlin continues to disappoint the media, which expect party leaders to be aggressive, noisy and unruly in the mode of Jean Chrétien. Media narratives, as we have shown, continue to code these behaviour patterns as the norm and insist that they are a sign of political competence. No wonder Jeffrey Simpson (1989) of the *Globe and Mail* speculates whether Audrey McLaughlin will be able to reject the aggressive demands of both the parliamentary system and the electronic media to follow her own preference for "grassroots politics" and coalition building. The debate continues on whether women's different attitudes to interaction and power are a result of different socialization and communication patterns for the two genders or of structural constraints. Apologists for the latter view argue that minority status in the political realm demands cunning and a consensus approach in order to get "women-friendly" legislation adopted against majority resistance (Lepsius 1990, 68). Whatever the reasons, there is good evidence that women politicians will have a leavening effect on Canadian party politics and prepare the ground for fashioning a new style of political sandbox that will be oriented to human needs.

Looking Toward the Future

Mary Collins, Minister of Immigration, when presenting her views on women in politics to a Royal Commission–sponsored symposium (Canada, Royal Commission 1990), compared the drive for equality to the income tax and noted that neither was very popular. She argued that, because there is no automatic progression from a male-dominated to an integrated politics in which women have an equal voice, the struggle must go on. Women, far from being a liability to Canadian parties in the 1990s, are in fact an asset. Women's variant attitudes toward power and privileges have a fresh appeal to Canadian voters, who have generally lost trust in politicians.

The question for the future is how to translate these differing outlooks into viable programs for institutional change and more women-friendly legislation? Political scientist Carol Mueller, exploring the historical development of women's political agendas, points out that two different strategies have been proposed (1988a, 291). One argues that equal rights are the best foundation for women's needs, the other contends that women have special needs with respect to their reproductive capacities and that "human difference" must, therefore, also be included in fashioning social legislation. By the late 1970s, American feminists involved in lobbying and litigation had discovered the limits of a strategy based on a literal interpretation of equal rights. In practice, equal rights turned out to mean nothing more than treating women like men, despite the differences in their objective circumstances. Wage equity was a virtually irrelevant principle in the face of pervasive occupational segregation. Women's health and child-care needs, the feminization of poverty and household violence could not be addressed in terms of strict gender equality (Costain 1988, 150–51). Increasingly, therefore, women's "specificity" became the benchmark for designing women-friendly legislation in the United States. During the same period, Canada, like Europe, also began to combine the two principles, passing the *Canadian Human Rights Act* (1977) while at the same time funding women's centres, women's research programs and abused women's transitional houses through Secretary of State grants (Armstrong 1990, 18).

Considerable argument continues over whether these initiatives resulted from what has been called the gender gap in voting. While women today outnumber men by about 7 percent in North American elections, it turns out that block voting as a pressure group is not very common. It appears primarily between well-educated working women and men at the middle and top ends of the occupational ladder, but not at all among lower socio-economic groups. Furthermore, such voting is issue specific in North America and Europe and manifests itself only on such topics as defence expenditures, abortion, social services and unemployment policies (Norris 1988, 223–28). A Canadian Advisory Council on the Status of Women background paper (Maillé 1990) notes that there is no conclusive data about the gender gap in Canada, although women have traditionally favoured the Liberal over the Conservative party by 10 percent. The reason for its nonemergence, Chantal Maillé suggests, is that Canadian women's groups have not yet succeeded in forming a distinct lobby to approach politicians with a single voice, as has been done by the National Organization of Women (NOW) south of the border (Costain 1988, 168–69).

It seems, however, that this may be remedied in the 1990s, because diverse women's groups have set up about 40 action committees across the country to recruit more women to run for office and to develop voting blocks around a welfare-state agenda, which today benefits women more than men (Maillé 1990, 26–30; Mueller 1988a, 299). Women's historical support for the Liberal rather than the Conservative party may, thus, be revived and become a new gender gap in the coming decade. What this says is that women's vote as a *potential* block vote will require Canadian parties to pay attention to women's welfare, peace and human-rights concerns in *substantial* rather than propagandistic ways. Social legislation based on both equality and specificity considerations highlights an ambivalence in feminist thinking, which will only be overcome by what Jill Vickers (1989, 32) calls a "double vision" for the future. Both the older concepts of service, duty and responsibility, and the newer ones of rights, entitlements and claims vis-à-vis society and the state will have to be accommodated in designing future, more women-friendly legislation. This also requires a reconceptualizing of the existing theory of justice to encompass both equality and equity, sameness and difference.

In looking toward the future, a final question that has been implicit in much of our argument now needs explicit confrontation. It concerns the state and women's relationship to it. On the one hand, we have argued that state institutions as they exist today are male designed and dominated, and therefore exhibit a culture that is difficult for women to penetrate and to live with. On the other, we have shown that Canadian feminists and others look to the state for policies and programs supporting women's special needs. The latter attitude implies that state institutions are malleable and open to change. Our evidence confirms that the women politicians we have talked to were generally of the opinion that state institutions *are* reformable. Each one of them has, with the help of supportive male colleagues, achieved some success in rectifying the disproportionate gradient of male influence.

This leads us to conclude that women in government *do* make a difference. The women ministers we talked to or whose biographies we consulted all have provided stepping-stones for improving women's condition: Claire Kirkland-Casgrain legally established married women's rights in Quebec; Monique Bégin introduced universal health insurance; Pat Carney provided for greater job equality in the federal bureaucracy; and Flora MacDonald inserted a women's equality clause into the latest *Broadcasting Act*. Second- and third-generation politicians like Audrey McLaughlin, Léa Cousineau, Chaviva Hošek and Sheila Copps, among others, are continuing this agenda. Extra commitment will be needed in the 1990s as women's issues are submerged in the North American economic recession. It is at these times that the growing number of feminist politicians among third-generation incumbents in municipal and provincial councils will make the greatest difference, for they will have the fresh ideas and, thus, will set the course for the future.

The possibility of transforming state institutions is also documented by Scandinavian women's groups, where much has already been achieved, and in Great Britain, where the Scottish Constitutional Convention of 1989 provided an opportunity for summarizing the latest ideas on redesigned state institutions. In a ringing manifesto, Scottish women's groups called for "user-friendly" institutions catering to the needs of everyone: women, men, immigrants of different ethnic backgrounds, the young and the old. Mary Fyfe, Labour MP from Glasgow Maryhill, defined user-friendliness in legislative institutions for politicians and constituents as "a normal working day, with time built in for constituency activities, time off to match school holidays and take account of family needs, adequate salaries with additional allowances for [careers], proper child-care and working facilities for members and their staff, procedures that would be *seen* to be fair, democratic, open and easily understood by newcomers, and a minimum of ritual" (Coote and Pattullo 1990, 275).

What the Scottish women were trying to do, in effect, was to import into the mainstream of representative democracy the political culture of the margins and the operating procedures of campaigns, social movements and community actions where women were already strong. These proposals for exercising power, and interacting with it, are much more in tune with everyday experience than anything that has ordinarily become associated with politics.

In such a redesigned system, socially responsible media will also be transformed and changed, because readers and viewers will demand a common reportorial focus and point of view for *all* public officials. Gone will be the reportage which deals with the presence of women in reductive terms, and gone also will be the stereotype-based media narrations that perpetuate a vision of women (in politics) based on gender *difference* rather than on equality, on strangeness rather than on parallel or similar interests. Furthermore, both the traditional and transitional narratives would have to shed their antisocial bias toward women and minority groups, which is manifested by not giving them credit for their contributions to public life.

Media personnel will also have to become mindful not to apply the four discriminatory narrative focuses and differential evaluation criteria discussed previously. These include the focus on a female incumbent's personal characteristics rather than on the substance of her statements and ignoring prior career activities, thereby making competence more difficult for her to establish. It would also no longer be considered fair to make a woman politician responsible for her gender nor to use the feminism label to discredit her as an individual, let alone to discredit the women's movement as a whole. Even-handed application of performance criteria on a uniform scale for women and men will also avoid the oppression of excellence as well as differential standards for female and male sexual behaviour.

Lest this scenario sound overly rosy, it is important to remember that social institutions are just that, socially constructed and therefore intimately related to changing social attitudes toward women's role in the public domain. These attitudes will undergo further pressures at home, during the recession, and abroad, as a result of the Eastern European migration and of the declining nation-state role as the 1992 European Economic unity project progresses. At this juncture, it is important to remember Rosemary Brown's admonition: "Women's most stubborn enemy [is] not misogyny but paternalism" (1989, 130). Male legislators in caucus and in Parliament continue to believe that they know better what women's needs are than women themselves. Since *overt* discrimination is no longer publicly condoned, this attitude leads to a strategy of passive resistance that is equally effective, because the male bias of political institutions is able to derail many female-sponsored initiatives. Angela Miles's dictum must therefore remain the guiding principle for concerned political women in the 1990s: "[We] must continue to insist on our right to participate fully in public life, but must at the same time challenge its very shape and underlying logic" (as quoted in Vickers 1989, 16).

RECOMMENDATIONS

1. One of the basic manifestations of discrimination against women resides in the ways in which the presence and role of women politicians are discussed. Therefore, we recommend that all sexist language be eliminated from government and public documents, namely the *Canada Elections Act.*

2. Women need to be informed and properly trained in order to make maximum use of information tools and the media to further their political endeavours. Women politicians have to be taught how the journalistic system works, how to answer questions and what the print and production values are. Therefore, we strongly encourage all Canadian political parties to offer a foundation course on media literacy in order for women within their ranks to become media wise, that is, to be able to deal more adequately with reportorial interviews, expectations and biases.

Similar courses are already available in certain universities, namely l'Université du Québec à Montréal, where women from different associations receive training specifically designed for their needs in relation to the media.

3. We are well aware that in the field of media, the notion of freedom of the press does not permit the implementation of restrictive rules concerning editorial policies. However, we believe that the media can be systematically invited to make better use of the human resources and women's political expertise presently available. It is also recommended that the media be invited to systematically cover women's progress, or activities within political parties, and to keep in touch with women's extra-state activities on all levels of politics: national, provincial, regional and municipal.

4. Since it has been established that women in key power positions have a direct influence on the presence of other women at all levels of an organization, concrete measures should be considered to break the "glass ceiling" beyond which women have not been able to advance. Therefore, we recommend that affirmative action programs be designed to promote women to top positions in media outlets and political parties.

5. We also believe that goodwill gestures on a symbolic level can have important effects. Such gestures can be triggered by actions that help to raise consciousness and create a climate of awareness and cooperation. The following recommendation deals with two such initiatives. We recommend the following:
    - that a national journalism prize be instituted, to be named after a prominent woman and adjudicated through the Canadian Advisory Council on the Status of Women in cooperation with journalists' associations. The aim of the competition would be to award a substantial monetary prize, to be sponsored by the Secretary of State, to the best media coverage of women's political activity during the year.
    - that the Secretary of State sponsor particular and specific research projects on the media coverage of women's political activities, both within parties and outside. Such sponsorship should, in particular, favour research projects dealing with women's political initiatives on the municipal level in Canada's large and middle-sized cities, where women already represent one-third of city councillors. Most new political initiatives will emerge on this level where women's issues (such as peace, the environment and the welfare state) are going to be highlighted.

APPENDIX
WOMEN POLITICIANS INTERVIEWED OR STUDIED
THROUGH BIOGRAPHICAL MATERIAL

First generation

Doris Anderson (ex-president of the Canadian Advisory Council on the Status of Women)

Monique Bégin (Liberal Party of Canada, former minister)

Rosemary Brown (NDP, British Columbia, leadership candidate)

Thérèse Casgrain (Co-operative Commonwealth Federation, Quebec, Senator; autobiography)

Judy Erola (Liberal Party of Canada, former minister)

Pauline Jewett (New Democratic Party of Canada, Chancellor of Carleton University)

Thérèse Lavoie-Roux (Liberal, Quebec, former minister)

Judy LaMarsh (Liberal Party of Canada, former minister; autobiography)

Flora MacDonald (Progressive Conservative Party of Canada, former minister)

Jeanne Sauvé (Liberal Party of Canada, former minister, Governor General; biography)

Second generation

Mary Collins (Progressive Conservative Party of Canada, minister responsible for the status of women and associate minister of national defence)

Sheila Copps (Liberal Party of Canada, leadership candidate; autobiography)

Francine Cosman (Liberal, Nova Scotia)

Léa Cousineau (president of the executive committee, City of Montreal)

Christine Hart (Liberal, Ontario, former minister)

Chaviva Hošek (Liberal, Ontario, former minister)

Thérèse Killens (Liberal Party of Canada)

Aldéa Landry (Liberal, New Brunswick, vice-premier)

Audrey McLaughlin (New Democratic Party of Canada, leader of the party)

Maureen McTeer (candidate in 1988 for the Progressive Conservative Party of Canada)

Third generation

Marlene Catterall (Liberal Party of Canada)

Dorothy Doley (PC, Saskatchewan)

Sheila Gervais (Liberal Party of Canada, secretary-general)

Shirley Maheu (Liberal Party of Canada)

Sandra Mitchell (NDP, Saskatchewan, president)

Louise O'Neill (candidate in 1988 for New Democratic Party of Canada)

Journalists and Academics Consulted

Nicole Bélanger (directrice régionale, Radio-Canada)

Gretta Chambers (Montreal *Gazette*)

Ami Lönnroth (*Svenska Dagbladet*)

Robert Mackenzie (*Toronto Star*)

Trina McQueen (director of CBC English Network)

Francine Pelletier (*La Presse*)

Carolle Simard (Department of Political Science, Université du Québec à Montréal)

BIBLIOGRAPHY

Allard, Carole-Marie. 1987. "Ottawa: les femmes emménagent." *Commerce* (October): 102–106.

Anderson, Doris. 1987. *To Change the World: A Biography of Pauline Jewett.* Richmond Hill: Irwin.

Armstrong, Sally. 1990. "A Lesson in Herstory." *Homemakers Magazine* (September): 11–26.

Bashevkin, Sylvia. 1983. "Social Change and Political Partisanship: The Development of Women's Attitudes in Quebec, 1965–79." *Comparative Political Studies* 16 (July): 147–72.

———. 1985. *Toeing the Lines: Women and Party Politics in English Canada.* Toronto: University of Toronto Press.

Bauch, Hubert. 1982. "Campagnolo: Can She Climb to PM's Job?" *Gazette* (Montreal), 13 November.

Booth, Amy. 1964. "A Striking Political Heroine Plans to Save Quebec Women from Their Medieval Bondage." *Financial Post*, 23 May.

Brodie, M. Janine. 1985. *Women and Politics in Canada.* Toronto: McGraw-Hill Ryerson.

Brodie, M. Janine, and Jill McCalla Vickers. 1982. *Canadian Women in Politics: An Overview.* CRIAW Papers No. 2. Ottawa: Canadian Research Institute for the Advancement of Women.

Brown, Rosemary. 1989. *Being Brown: A Very Public Life.* Toronto: Random House.

Burt, Sandra, Lorraine Code and Lindsay Dorney, eds. 1988. *Changing Patterns: Women in Canada.* Toronto: McClelland and Stewart.

Camp, Dalton. 1989. "Let's Treat Audrey Like One of the Boys." *Toronto Star,* 6 December.

Canada. Royal Commission on the Status of Women. 1970. *Report.* Ottawa: Information Canada.

Canada. Royal Commission on Electoral Reform and Party Financing. 1990. Symposium on Women's Participation in Political Parties, held in Montreal, 31 October–2 November.

Casgrain, Thérèse. 1972. *A Woman in a Man's World.* Trans. Joyce Marshall. Toronto: McClelland and Stewart. (Originally published in French as *Une femme chez les hommes.* Montreal: Éditions du jour, 1971.)

Christy, Carol A. 1987. *Sex Differences in Political Participation: Processes of Change in Fourteen Nations.* New York: Praeger.

Clarke, Harold D., and Allan Kornberg. 1979. "Moving up the Political Escalator: Women Party Officials in the United States and Canada." *Journal of Politics* 41 (May): 442–77.

Cohen, Yolande. 1989. *Women and Counter-Power.* Montreal: Black Rose Press.

Coote, Anna, and Polly Pattullo. 1990. *Power and Prejudice: Women and Politics.* London: Weidenfeld and Nicolson.

Copps, Sheila. 1986. *Nobody's Baby.* Toronto: Deneau.

Cornacchia, Cheryl. 1990. "Pressing on: Women's Perspective Important to the News." *Gazette* (Montreal), 19 November.

Costain, Anne N. 1988. "Women's Claims as a Special Interest." In *The Politics of the Gender Gap,* ed. Carol Mueller. Beverly Hills: Sage Publications.

Crean, Susan. 1987. "Piecing the Picture Together: Women and the Media in Canada." *Canadian Woman Studies* 8 (Spring): 15–21.

Curran, Peggy. 1989. "Yukon Hopes McLaughlin Win Boosts the Great White North." *Gazette* (Montreal), 9 December.

Descarries, Francine, and Shirley Roy. 1988. *Le mouvement des femmes et ses courants de pensée: essai de typologie.* CRIAW Papers No. 19. Ottawa: Canadian Research Institute for the Advancement of Women.

Eichler, Margrit. 1980. *The Double Standard: A Feminist Critique of Feminist Social Science*. London: Croom Helm.

Epstein, Cynthia Fuchs, and Rose Coser, eds. 1981. *Access to Power: Cross-National Studies of Women and Elites*. London: George Allen and Unwin.

Evans, Sara. 1979. *Personal Politics*. New York: Vintage Books.

Fraser, Graham. 1989. "Bye, Mr. Broadbent; Hello There, Audrey." *Globe and Mail*, 9 December.

Friedan, Betty. 1963. *The Feminine Mystique*. New York: Dell.

Frizzell, Alan, and Anthony Westell. 1989. "The Media and the Campaign." In Alan Frizzell, Jon Pammett and Anthony Westell, *The Canadian General Election of 1988*. Ottawa: Carleton University Press.

Fruman, Leslie. 1984. "Lucie Pépin Is a Proven Feminist." *Toronto Star*, 7 December.

Gazette (Montreal). 1975. "Tough Woman Tory Has Skill to Be Party Leader, Next PM." 5 February.

———. 1990. "TV Downplays Women on, off Screen: Study." 21 November.

Gillett, Margaret, and Kay Sibbald, eds. 1984. *A Fair Shake: Autobiographical Essays by McGill Women*. Montreal: Eden Press.

Githens, Marianne, and Jewel Prestage. 1977. *A Portrait of Marginality*. New York: David McKay.

Goyette, Linda. 1986. "'Big Federal Win' a Modest Step into Power Circle." *Edmonton Journal*, 20 April.

Gray, Charlotte. 1989. "The New F-Word." *Saturday Night* (April): 17–20.

Grewe-Partsch, Marianne. 1990. "Changing Understandings of Women's Political Values in the Federal Republic of Germany." In *Women and Power: Canadian and German Experiences*, ed. Gertrude J. Robinson and Dieta Sixt. Montreal: McGill Studies in Communications and Goethe-Institut Montreal.

Gzowski, Peter. 1962. "The New Women in Politics." *Maclean's*, 21 April, 30–31, 52–54.

Hamilton, Roberta, and Michele Barrett, eds. 1987. *The Politics of Diversity: Feminism, Marxism and Nationalism*. Montreal: Book Centre.

Hochschild, Arlie, and Anne Machung. 1990. *The Second Shift: Inside the Two-Job Marriage*. New York: Avon Books.

Hošek, Chaviva. 1989. "How Women Fought for Equality." In *Women and Men: Interdisciplinary Readings on Gender*, ed. Greta Hofmann Nemiroff. Toronto: Fitzhenry and Whiteside.

Jeffrey, Liss. 1989. "Waiting for the Results." *Scan* (March/April): 7–10.

————. 1990. "Women and the Media in Canada: A Question of Cultural Authority." In *Women and Power: Canadian and German Experiences,* ed. Gertrude J. Robinson and Dieta Sixt. Montreal: McGill Studies in Communications and Goethe-Institut Montreal.

Kaihla, Paul. 1990. "Battling the Odds: Six Liberals with Hope in Their Hearts." *Maclean's,* 5 February, 28–29.

Kay, Barry, R.D. Lambert, S.D. Brown and J.A. Curtis. 1987. "Gender and Political Activity in Canada, 1965–1984." *Canadian Journal of Political Science* 20:851–63.

Kealey, Linda, and Joan Sangster, eds. 1989. *Beyond the Vote: Canadian Women and Politics.* Toronto: University of Toronto Press.

Kieran, Sheila H. 1968. "Who's Downgrading Women? Women." *Maclean's* (August): 18–19, 40–42.

Knoke, David. 1984. "Conceptual and Measurement Aspects in the Study of Political Generations." *Journal of Political and Military Sociology* 12 (Spring): 191–201.

Kornberg, Allan, and Norman Thomas. 1965. "The Political Socialization of National Legislative Elites in the United States and Canada." *Journal of Politics* 27:761–75.

LaMarsh, Judy. 1968. *Memoirs of a Bird in a Gilded Cage.* Toronto: McClelland and Stewart.

Laplante, Norman. 1990. "The Sauvés: In the Service of the Nation." *The Archivist* 17 (May/June): 2–4.

Lavigne, Marie. 1990. "Femmes et pouvoir politique: une intégration à réussir." In *Women and Power: Canadian and German Experiences,* ed. Gertrude J. Robinson and Dieta Sixt. Montreal: McGill Studies in Communications and Goethe-Institut Montreal.

Lee, Robert Mason. 1989a. *One Hundred Monkeys: The Triumph of Popular Wisdom in Canadian Politics.* Toronto: Macfarlane Walter and Ross.

————. 1989b. "Sorry, Mo." *Saturday Night* (October): 63–69.

Lepsius, Renate. 1990. "Women Politicians in the Bundestag: How to Design 'Women-friendly' Policies." In *Women and Power: Canadian and German Experiences,* ed. Gertrude J. Robinson and Dieta Sixt. Montreal: McGill Studies in Communications and Goethe-Institut Montreal.

MacBeth-Williams, Tannis, D. Baron, S. Philips, L. Travis and D. Jackson. 1986. "The Portrayal of Sex Roles on Canadian and U.S. Television." Paper presented at a conference of the International Association for Mass Communication Research, New Delhi.

Maclean's. 1990. "Life at the Top: Thatcher Relishes Her Hard-Edged Image." 3 December, 40–41.

Maillé, Chantal. 1990. *Primed for Power: Women in Canadian Politics.* Ottawa: Canadian Advisory Council on the Status of Women.

Mannheim, Karl. 1952. "The Problem of Generations." In *Essays on the Sociology of Knowledge,* ed. Paul Kecskemeti. New York: Oxford University Press.

Meyrowitz, Joshua. 1985. *No Sense of Place: The Impact of Electronic Media on Social Behavior.* New York: Oxford University Press.

Mueller, Carol M. 1988a. "Continuity and Change in Women's Political Agenda." In *The Politics of the Gender Gap,* ed. Carol Mueller. Beverly Hills: Sage Publications.

———. 1988b. "The Empowerment of Women: Polling and the Women's Voting Bloc." In *The Politics of the Gender Gap,* ed. Carol Mueller. Beverly Hills: Sage Publications.

Norris, Pippa. 1988. "The Gender Gap: A Cross-National Trend?" In *The Politics of the Gender Gap,* ed. Carol Mueller. Beverly Hills: Sage Publications.

La Presse. 1962. "Un ministre bien chapeauté: Madame Ellen Fairclough." 18 January.

Robin, Marie-Jeanne. 1983. *La politique au féminin.* Interview with Thérèse Lavoie-Roux. Montreal: Inédi.

Robinson, Gertrude Joch. 1975. "Women Journalists in Canadian Dailies: A Social and Professional Profile." *McGill Working Papers in Communications.* Montreal: McGill University.

———. 1978. "Women, Media Access and Social Control." In *Women and the News,* ed. Laurily Keir Epstein. New York: Hastings House.

Robinson, Gertrude Joch, and Dieta Sixt, eds. 1990. *Women and Power: Canadian and German Experiences.* Montreal: McGill Studies in Communications and Goethe-Institut Montreal.

Saint-Jean, Armande. 1990. "Les femmes et l'information: Une perspective québécoise." In *Women and Power: Canadian and German Experiences,* ed. Gertrude J. Robinson and Dieta Sixt. Montreal: McGill Studies in Communications and Goethe-Institut Montreal.

Schneider, Beth E. 1988. "Political Generations and the Contemporary Women's Movement." *Sociological Inquiry* 58(1): 4–21.

Sears, Val. 1983. "Janis Johnson: High Profile." *Toronto Star,* 22 November.

Simpson, Jeffrey. 1989. "From the Crucible, a Determined Pro." *Globe and Mail*, 4 December.

Stacey, Judith, and Barrie Thorne. 1985. "The Missing Feminist Revolution in Sociology." *Social Problems* 32(4): 301–16.

Tuchman, Gaye. 1972. "Objectivity as Strategic Ritual: An Examination of Newsmen's Notions of Objectivity." *American Journal of Sociology* 77:660–79.

———. 1978. *Making News: A Study in the Construction of Reality.* New York: Free Press.

Vickers, Jill McCalla. 1989. "Feminist Approaches to Women in Politics." In *Beyond the Vote: Canadian Women and Politics*, ed. Linda Kealey and Joan Sangster. Toronto: University of Toronto Press.

Vickers, Jill McCalla, and June Adam. 1977. *But Can You Type?* Toronto: Clarke Irwin.

Walker, Robert. 1990. "In Byline Game Men Win 67–30: National Study Suggests Gazette Ratio Is Typical." *Gazette* (Montreal), 24 September.

Winsor, Hugh. 1989. "Keen Organization and Networking Compensated for Lacklustre Speech." *Globe and Mail*, 4 December.

Woods, Shirley E. 1986. *Her Excellency Jeanne Sauvé.* Toronto: Macmillan of Canada.

CONTRIBUTORS TO VOLUME 6

Sylvia Bashevkin   University of Toronto
Janine Brodie   York University
Lynda Erickson   Simon Fraser University
Gertrude J. Robinson   McGill University
Armande Saint-Jean   Université du Québec à Montréal
Lisa Young   Research Analyst, RCERPF

ACKNOWLEDGEMENTS

The Royal Commission on Electoral Reform and Party Financing and the publishers wish to acknowledge with gratitude the permission of the following publishers and individuals to reprint and translate material from their works:

The Globe and Mail; M.G.A. Agency Inc.; Charlotte Gray; Random House of Canada Ltd.; The Toronto Star Syndicate.

Care has been taken to trace the ownership of copyright material used in the text, including the tables and figures. The authors and publishers welcome any information enabling them to rectify any reference or credit in subsequent editions.

Consistent with the Commission's objective of promoting full participation in the electoral system by all segments of Canadian society, gender neutrality has been used wherever possible in the editing of the research studies.

THE COLLECTED RESEARCH STUDIES*

---

* The titles of studies may not be final in all cases.

SYLVIA BASHEVKIN	Women's Participation in Political Parties
LISA YOUNG	Legislative Turnover and the Election of Women to the Canadian House of Commons
LYNDA ERICKSON	Women and Candidacies for the House of Commons
GERTRUDE J. ROBINSON AND ARMANDE SAINT-JEAN, WITH THE ASSISTANCE OF CHRISTINE RIOUX	Women Politicians and Their Media Coverage: A Generational Analysis

VOLUME 7
Ethno-Cultural Groups and Visible Minorities in Canadian Politics: The Question of Access
Kathy Megyery, Editor

DAIVA K. STASIULIS AND YASMEEN ABU-LABAN	The House the Parties Built: (Re)constructing Ethnic Representation in Canadian Politics
ALAIN PELLETIER	Politics and Ethnicity: Representation of Ethnic and Visible-Minority Groups in the House of Commons
CAROLLE SIMARD	Visible Minorities and the Canadian Political System

VOLUME 8
Youth in Canadian Politics: Participation and Involvement
Kathy Megyery, Editor

RAYMOND HUDON, BERNARD FOURNIER AND LOUIS MÉTIVIER, WITH THE ASSISTANCE OF BENOÎT-PAUL HÉBERT	To What Extent Are Today's Young People Interested in Politics? An Inquiry among 16- to 24-Year-Olds
PATRICE GARANT	The Possibilities of Reopening the Voting Age Issue under the *Charter of Rights and Freedoms*
JON H. PAMMETT AND JOHN MYLES	Lowering the Voting Age to 16

VOLUME 9

Aboriginal Peoples and Electoral Reform in Canada
  Robert A. Milen, Editor

ROBERT A. MILEN	Aboriginal Constitutional and Electoral Reform
AUGIE FLERAS	Aboriginal Electoral Districts for Canada: Lessons from New Zealand
VALERIE ALIA	Aboriginal Peoples and Campaign Coverage in the North
ROGER GIBBINS	Electoral Reform and Canada's Aboriginal Population: An Assessment of Aboriginal Electoral Districts

VOLUME 10

Democratic Rights and Electoral Reform in Canada
  Michael Cassidy, Editor

JENNIFER SMITH	The Franchise and Theories of Representative Government
PIERRE LANDREVILLE AND LUCIE LEMONDE	Voting Rights for Inmates
YVES DENONCOURT	Reflections concerning Criteria for the Vote for Persons with Mental Disorders
PATRICE GARANT	Political Rights of Public Servants in the Political Process
KENNETH KERNAGHAN	The Political Rights of Canada's Federal Public Servants
PETER MCCORMICK	Provision for the Recall of Elected Officials: Parameters and Prospects
DAVID MAC DONALD	Referendums and Federal General Elections
JOHN C. COURTNEY AND DAVID E. SMITH	Registering Voters: Canada in a Comparative Context
CÉCILE BOUCHER	Administration and Enforcement of the Elections Act in Canada

VOLUME 11

Drawing the Map: Equality and Efficacy of the Vote in Canadian Electoral Boundary Reform
David Small, Editor

VOLUME 12

Political Ethics: A Canadian Perspective
Janet Hiebert, Editor

VOLUME 23
Canadian Political Parties in the Constituencies:
A Local Perspective

R. KENNETH CARTY   Canadian Political Parties in the
                                    Constituencies: A Local Perspective

COMMISSION ORGANIZATION

CHAIRMAN
Pierre Lortie

COMMISSIONERS
Pierre Fortier
Robert Gabor
William Knight
Lucie Pépin

SENIOR OFFICERS

Executive Director
Guy Goulard

Director of Research
Peter Aucoin

Special Adviser to the Chairman
Jean-Marc Hamel

Research
F. Leslie Seidle,
   Senior Research Coordinator

Coordinators
Herman Bakvis
Michael Cassidy
Frederick J. Fletcher
Janet Hiebert
Kathy Megyery
Robert A. Milen
David Small

Assistant Coordinators
David Mac Donald
Cheryl D. Mitchell

Legislation
Jules Brière, Senior Adviser
Gérard Bertrand
Patrick Orr

Communications and Publishing
Richard Rochefort, Director
Hélène Papineau, Assistant
   Director
Paul Morisset, Editor
Kathryn Randle, Editor

Finance and Administration
Maurice R. Lacasse, Director

Contracts and Personnel
Thérèse Lacasse, Chief

Editorial, Design and Production Services

Printed and bound in Canada by
Best Gagné Book Manufacturers